21 DAYS
of
BREAKTHROUGH
PRAYER

The Power of Agreement

JIM MAXIM
with *Cathy Maxim* and *Daniel Henderson*

WHITAKER
HOUSE

21 DAYS OF BREAKTHROUGH PRAYER:
The Power of Agreement

acts413.net
strategicrenewal.com/21days

ISBN: 978-1-64123-076-6
eBook ISBN: 978-1-64123-077-3
Printed in the United States of America
© 2018 by Jim Maxim

Whitaker House
1030 Hunt Valley Circle
New Kensington, PA 15068
www.whitakerhouse.com

Special printing for *World Magazine*.

Dedication

This book is dedicated to all of the pastors who labor in God's vineyard to strengthen His saints. Our desire is for this book to be a tool to assist pastors in mobilizing their churches in the renewal of corporate and personal prayer.

Contents

Foreword

Prayer is the source of the Christian life, a Christian's life-line. As I wrote in my book *Fresh Wind, Fresh Fire*, "Otherwise, it's like having a baby in your arms and dressing her up so cute—but she's not breathing! Never mind the frilly clothes; *stabilize the child's vital signs*." We all need the Spirit's help and practical encouragement to make prayer the vital organ God intended it to be in our lives.

As we grow in prayer, we soon learn that one of the most important areas of focus is that of praying for church leaders. The apostle Paul often implored the early churches to pray for him. (See Romans 15:30–33; Ephesians 6:19; Colossians 4:3; 1 Thessalonians 5:25; 2 Thessalonians 3:1.) If the great apostle needed prayer, how much more do today's church leaders need our intercessory support? Pastoring in the twenty-first century means facing immense and often mean-spirited challenges. The best thing we can do for our leaders is not to scold them, or even take them out for Sunday dinner. What is better by far is to pray for them, daily and fervently.

I am grateful for this valuable resource compiled by my friends Jim and Cathy Maxim and Daniel Henderson. This guide will inspire your prayer life through the daily readings and the accompanying audio prayers. Beyond this, you will be equipped to pray effectively for your church leaders with biblical understanding and Christian love.

Jim Maxim is a successful businessman with an extraordinary passion for prayer. He mobilizes pastors to pray together and leads citywide gatherings of powerful intercession on behalf of church leaders through his Acts 413 Ministries. Pastor Daniel Henderson and I have partnered together to challenge our pastoral colleagues all across America to lead their churches in prayer. Daniel and I partner in a fellowship of praying pastors. The 6:4 Fellowship calls church leaders to make prayer and the ministry of the Word truly vital in their lives and churches.

In this helpful volume, Jim, his wife Cathy, and Daniel have combined their passion and teaching to give you an essential "kick-start" in your prayer life, leading to a deeper conviction about praying for your church and ministry leaders. I am thankful for the friendship of these treasured brothers and sister, and I know that this new tool will help you to honor Christ as you experience a greater focus and fruitfulness in your life of prayer.

—*Pastor Jim Cymbala*
The Brooklyn Tabernacle

Introduction

Are there things in your personal life, your loved ones' lives, or your church life that need to change for the better? Are you ready to discover a real breakthrough in these challenging situations? Have you ever considered that God is just waiting for His people to cry out to Him in prayer together?

The prayer of agreement is one of the most powerful gifts that God has provided for victory in our Christian lives. Jesus Himself boldly proclaimed, *"Again I say to you that if two of you agree on earth concerning anything that they ask, it will be done for them by My Father in heaven. For where two or three are gathered together in My name, I am there in the midst of them"* (Matthew 18:19–20).

God has declared that His power resides in the center of our prayers of agreement. God is our Father, and we can always go to Him in prayer. But He strongly encourages us to pray with one another in powerful agreeing prayer. God has promised us that He will respond to this time of focused prayer as we seek His face together. Second Chronicles 7:14 says, *"If My people who are called by My name will humble themselves, and pray and seek My face, and turn from their wicked ways, then I will hear from heaven, and **will forgive their sin and heal their land**."*

Thankfully, anyone who is already God's son or daughter has the privilege to spend time with Him in prayer any day at any time. But during this next twenty-one days, things will be very different as we go to God together and experience a time of intimacy and intercession that will forever change the way we pray, think, and act regarding the gift of prayer.

During these twenty-one days, you will see a dynamic change in your personal prayer life and in the prayer life of your church. You will discover the power in the prayer of agreement and how it will bless you and those you love for eternity. More can be accomplished through prayer than all the efforts in our own strength!

How can you participate in these twenty-one days of prayer? We have made this prayer time interactive so that you can read through it with a prayer partner to agree with you for God's answers. At the end of each devotional reading, you can visit www.acts413.net and join me (Jim Maxim), Cathy Maxim, and Daniel Henderson in a powerful time of agreeing prayer. We will enter God's presence together daily, praying for the power of the Holy Spirit to sweep through your circumstances with the breakthrough that you need in your life and the lives of those you love.

Daniel, Cathy, and I are convinced that this next twenty-one days of prayer will be a defining moment in your relationship with God. It will change your personal life because your "Dad," God Almighty, is going to wrap His arms around you in a way that you need right now or that you have never experienced before. Together, we will go before His throne with your prayer concerns and your loved ones'. We will take Him at His Word and enter into the intimacy He has reserved for all His family. We will learn to pray the Scriptures together by the leading of the Holy Spirit. As God's people, when we recognize that He is not only true to His word, but also that He *is* His Word, we will begin to see what prayer can really do!

We will also pray earnestly together for our pastors and their families. We will lift the "shield of faith" over them and call their names out before almighty God, asking Him to bless, encourage, and strengthen them. Our pastors are under tremendous attack in today's culture, and they need our prayers and encouragement in every area of their lives. God will be very pleased with His church as we selflessly take this time to intercede for them. Remember, a healthy pastor is a healthy church. A healthy church changes the world!

Each day of prayer will be different as we focus on a particular Scripture, on an area of fellowship with God, on prayer concerns and spiritual encouragement. Our desire is for you to enter into a life of communion with your heavenly Father; with Jesus, His Son; and with the Holy Spirit. We pray earnestly for God's presence in your life to be so contagious that He will use your newfound passion for prayer to ignite your pastor, your church, your personal life, and your loved ones, setting them all on fire for His glory!

Please join us on this twenty-one-day journey as we enter God's presence and discover the limitless power of the prayer of agreement to bring change in our lives for eternity.

—*Jim and Cathy Maxim and Daniel Henderson*

Join the Interactive
21 Days of Breakthrough Prayer
Experience!

To help you in this prayer journey, go online to access a daily playlist of prayers to be used alongside this book.

Here's how it works:

+ Read the devotional for that day.
+ Go online to **www.acts413.net/21days** or **www.strategic renewal.com/21days** and listen to the corresponding prayers for that day.
+ Pray in agreement with us for the Almighty to *break through* in your life for His glory and for your good.
+ Share this resource with your brothers and sisters in Christ that we all might agree.

Our hope is that this will be a powerful tool to change your prayer life and help usher you in to the daily presence of God.

Part 1: Background

Chapter 1

Prayer in the Church:
A Tale of Two Ships

"Isn't it possible that prayer is the missing link that
God has provided for us?"
—*Jim Maxim*

Two ships of the same size leave the harbor and head out to sea. They sail off in the same direction, but then one of them begins to veer off course, listing starboard, moving in a different direction.

From the bow, both ships seem to be identical, like many churches today. They have the same departments; each has a worship team, a children's program, a youth ministry, nursery facilities, a sanctuary, pastors' offices, a café, and so forth. Each reaches out to the community, sponsors missions trips, holds Bible teaching conferences, and uses state-of-the-art media technology. The people even seem to be dressed similarly.

However, looking at the ships' port and starboard sides reveals that they are not identical after all. One ship has a prayer room that is relegated to a small corner in the stern. Although this ship seems to have more glitter than the other, there are many things weighing it down—things that look rusted, old, and decayed—and causing it to veer off course. Barnacles are clinging to the sides, slowly and imperceptibly damaging the hull. All of the passengers on board are going about their business as usual with a casual attitude, maybe a little arrogantly or just wrapped up in what they are doing, making decisions on the fly.

The second ship has all the same departments as the first ship, but along the entire length of its decks, people are praying to God, calling out to Him, worshipping Him, and asking Him to shower His presence upon them. Some of the people are prostrate, while others are on their knees, sitting down, or standing. All of them are in prayer and are actively waiting upon the Lord. They are hungering for Him with intensity, and their attitude permeates the entire ship.

This ship is cutting through the waters faster and with greater ease than the first ship, even though the waves are hitting it more intensely. No glitter, no barnacles, no rust—yet moving swiftly through the rougher waves.

The question the Lord is laying on my heart to ask pastors and their congregations is this: Which ship would you like to be on?

THE CHALLENGE OF PRAYER

Why is prayer so hard? Why don't we as the church of Jesus Christ take prayer as seriously as Jesus did? Why do many of us say we pray and say we believe that God answers prayer but, for the most part, do not participate in corporate prayer meetings? Why don't we want to gather together as a body of believers and honestly ask and believe God to answer our prayers? After all, the church was born in a prayer meeting in the upper room.

I know that pastors often will not ask their congregations to meet regularly to seek God together in prayer because they know people will not find the time to come. It brings me to a very puzzling question: Why has the privilege of corporate prayer become so unattractive to Christians?

I honestly believe that, most of the time, our level of expectation for God to truly intervene is low—so low that we expect God to answer only the prayers that we can almost fulfill ourselves! That doesn't take much faith! One of the reasons it's almost impossible for churches in America to have a good response to their prayer meetings is because most Christians do not believe that God answers prayers that move mountains. (See Matthew 17:20.)

Can you imagine what a church body that met regularly and sought the face of God with a humble and contrite heart would look like? Doesn't God say that He will not ignore a broken spirit and humble and contrite heart? (See Psalm 51:17.) Ignorance of the outcomes of prayer is probably the number one reason churches do not enter into the magnificent gift and privilege of praying together. Throughout the Bible, God encourages us to embrace the power of prayer to change everything in our lives:

> *If My people who are called by My name will humble themselves, and pray and seek My face, and turn from their wicked ways, then will I hear from heaven, and **will forgive their sin and heal their land**.*   (2 Chronicles 7:14)

> *Now this is the confidence that we have in Him, that if we ask anything according to His will, He hears us. And if we know that He hears us, whatever we ask, we know that **we have the petitions that we have asked of Him**.*
> (1 John 5:14–15)

> *When you pray, go into your room, and when you have shut your door, pray to your Father who is in the secret place; and*

> *your Father who sees in secret will reward you openly.*
>
> (Matthew 6:6)

If we believe that these Scriptures are true, then why is prayer, personally and corporately, not of vital importance in our lives? Do you understand a little better why God's most powerful servants have said that they wish they would have prayed more and led others with them in prayer?

Perhaps prayer is the missing link that God has provided for us. With prayer, we will enter a new dimension in our walk with Him. With prayer, if we enter His gates with thanksgiving, the church of Jesus Christ will experience a powerful spiritual wave of His presence. I believe the destiny God has for each of us will start to unfold rapidly when we submit our heart and soul to Him for His eternal purposes in our lives. I pray that you would accept the awesome privilege of talking with God and receiving from Him the majesty of His presence in prayer.

> The Church is looking for better methods; God is looking for better men…. The Holy Ghost does not flow through methods, but through men. He does not come on machinery, but on men…men of prayer.[1]

PRAYER GETS PUSHED AWAY

For over forty years, I have observed that prayer gets pushed off the agenda. We get too busy or we just do not learn how much power prayer has to change our circumstances. Busyness and success occupy the church's life; before long, prayer is no longer a

---

1. Edward M. Bounds, *Power Through Prayer* (Racine, WI: Treasures Media, Inc., 2007), 2.

priority. Most pastors try hard to change this, but it is difficult to get the church to respond.

I have spoken to many pastors with a seminary education who confirm that the "practice" of prayer was never modeled to them by any professor. Prayer was just another theological subject, and the powerful importance of prayer was never conveyed as a top priority. As a result, when the local church experiences some success, the pastor and staff will often forget the emphasis on prayer in Jesus's life to fulfill the Father's will. When pastors lack fellowship with God in prayer, discouragement, anxiety, and ministry burnout set in. The work is on man's shoulders instead of God's. People with good intentions replace kingdom power with earthly principles.

Through this time of seeking God in intercessory prayer, we will pray for our pastors and their own personal prayer lives, encouraging them to lay the burdens of the church on God in prayer. We will also pray for the Holy Spirit to breathe life into the prayer lives of our congregations. God has promised. He can and will bring change to our lives as we seek His face in earnest together!

WE HAVE BEEN CHOSEN

We have been chosen by God, pastors and lay believers alike, as the means for the world to see His love in action. We are all the church, and we can all be used by God to reach out to the people in need of God's saving grace. We are the ones who will determine which ship we will board. Will you be on the ship whose passengers dedicate their lives to prayer and believe God for great things to happen through His kingdom? We have the awesome privilege to be used every day for God's glory!

Chapter 2
Personal Prayer: Nobody Is Beyond God's Reach

"The Gospel cannot live, fight, conquer without
prayer—prayer unceasing, instant and ardent."[2]
—E. M. Bounds

"Behold, the LORD's hand is not
so short that it cannot save;
nor is His ear so dull that it cannot hear."
—Isaiah 59:1 (NASB)

Prayer in the church is important; prayer in our personal lives is just as vital. The greatest miracles I have seen in my life are the ones that I knew with all my heart were not possible—the trial could not be overcome, the person could not be healed, the loved one could not be set free—without God Almighty stepping in and doing it. To actually see the hand of God move on my behalf is the deepest and most fulfilling thing I have ever experienced next to watching Him use me to bring someone else to Christ. That's why the people in Jerusalem said that the early Christians were men who "*have turned the world upside down*" (Acts 17:6). The people of that day actually saw the hand of God do incredible things, and He did it through ordinary people, like you and me. That same God, your Father, is doing the same things today.

---

2. Edward McKendree Bounds, *Purpose in Prayer* (New York: Fleming H. Revell Company, 1920), 72.

Do you long to see those you love enter into a deep and genuine relationship with Jesus? Do you have loved ones who are in some type of bondage that just looks hopeless? Have you begun to have serious doubts that they will ever change? Have you spoken for years with certain people and the fact that God loves them just doesn't seem to get through?

PRAYER UNLOCKS HEAVEN'S DOOR

Prayer is the most powerful force known to man, so why don't we want to turn to prayer to answer the problems in the lives of those we love? We should be quick to pray in the supernatural before we try to do anything in the natural. Prayer wields the power that unlocks heaven's doors and brings the answers that you desire for you, your family, your pastor, and your church.

Prayer is laying hold of the unseen reality that lies before us. Prayer is accepting the rights and privileges of a citizen of heaven. Prayer is declaring once again that God is mighty and that He has our lives in the palm of His hands. Prayer is the method God chose to align our spirits with His. Oswald Chambers' life was focused on prayer. That is why he declared, "Prayer does not *fit* us for the greater work; prayer **is** the greater work."

The fact is that prayer is the hardest work we will ever do… and the most rewarding.

PRAYER HAS NO BARRIERS

If you have faith as a mustard seed, you will say unto this mountain, "Move from here to there," and it will move; and nothing will be impossible for you. (Matthew 17:20)

I have seen from personal experience that prayer has no barriers, not even thirty thousand feet in the air. Let me share a story with you.

I boarded an early morning flight a couple of years ago, as I had done hundreds of times before, only this time, I witnessed one of the greatest miracles I have ever seen. As I walked through the plane's doorway, the flight attendant said, "Good morning," and I headed toward my seat.

Walking down the aisle, I was shocked to see only one other passenger on the plane. It was another man, and he was sitting in the very last row. I was dumbfounded—a completely empty jet! Puzzled, I took my seat and thought about my customary morning prayer time. Early that morning, I had lifted up a simple prayer, as I did at the start of each day: "Father God, in the name of Jesus, please use me today to make faith come alive in someone's heart, somewhere. Lord, please help me share Your love with somebody today."

My first thought was that God had emptied an entire flight so that the man in the back of the plane could hear about Jesus's love for him. I was so excited that I could hardly wait to get back there, introduce myself, and start some small talk with him. I looked forward to seeing how the Holy Spirit would lead this encounter.

The plane reached cruising altitude, and I started to take off my seatbelt, restless to begin talking with the other man. At that point, the flight attendant walked up and very politely asked me if there was anything she could get for me. I said, "No, thanks."

"Would you like some breakfast?"

"No, thank you," I answered once again. Not to be put off, she asked me a third time if I wanted any coffee or orange juice.

I started to get a little annoyed. After all, I had a God-ordained appointment with the man in the back, and she was distracting me. Suddenly, it was as if the Holy Spirit hit me on the back of the head and said, "It's not him, Jim; it's her!"

I'm sure that my eyes widened about two inches and my mouth dropped open. With a completely different expression, I responded, "I think I'll have some coffee, and while you're at it, I'll take some orange juice, as well!" As she turned to walk away, I felt God's overwhelming presence and quickly started praying. Sometimes, sharing the gospel with a woman when I am by myself can be tricky, and I am careful to rely on the Lord. When I am sure God has ordained the moment, I get all green lights and move forward in faith. I knew in my spirit that this young woman had been marked by God to hear His message of love and forgiveness today, right now, on this plane, at thirty thousand feet!

When she returned with the coffee, she asked me if I had my own business, and I answered her briefly. Then to open the conversation about the Lord, I said, "I'm very thankful for the way things have turned out and how God has blessed me with a beautiful wife and three sons." I saw the "look" come over her, as I have seen it come over others so many times before. It's the look that tells me someone is reflecting very deeply in their own hearts. I spoke again: "I bet you have a lot of things to be thankful for." Right then, she just stopped. It was as if she was frozen in time. Her eyes closed, and tears started flowing down her cheeks like Niagara Falls.

"You have a mother at home praying for you, don't you?" I asked quietly. "It's time to come home today. God has emptied this entire plane and rearranged the airline's schedule just for you." God's presence and the power of His love were so strong, I knew He was standing right there with us.

"You've been running long enough," I continued. "It's time to surrender to His love for you." She just kept on weeping, and I was watching the greatest miracle in the kingdom of heaven. I knew her mother's prayers were being answered right before my eyes.

It was one of the holiest moments of my life. God Himself had reached down from heaven and wrapped His arms around this young woman and was showering His love, peace, and forgiveness all over her, and I was privileged to have a front-row seat for it all. I sat there in holy reverence, reflecting on His unending love. Nobody, absolutely nobody, is beyond God's reach.

I prayed with the flight attendant right then, and she rededicated her life to Jesus, promising to get back into God's Word and Christian fellowship. I assured her that if God could empty a plane to get to her, He was more than capable of directing her everyday life! I encouraged her to call her mother as soon as we landed. What joy there would be in that phone call!

Later, I walked off the plane in humble amazement. I sat alone in the airport terminal for a while, reflecting on the miracle that had just occurred—the almighty God had emptied an entire aircraft in response to one mother's fervent prayers!

This was the outcome of her mother's faith and prayer in action. Prayer was the activity that put me there that day! The almighty God was responding to prayer, a calling out to God in obedience to His Word, to bring this young woman home again. A mother's cry to the almighty God never goes unnoticed.

This story continually reminds me that God will do absolutely whatever it takes to bring a person to a place to receive His love if we will only pray. Praise His holy name! Even at 30,000 feet in the air, God had it all prepared for her, and all she had to do was receive it. This is the supernatural power of prayer. This is what happens when we take God at His Word.

Brothers and sisters, please don't miss the importance of God's call to prayer. He has given prayer to us as a privilege and an extraordinary gift. In the next twenty-one days, as we take God at His Word and start daily in the throne room of almighty God, we will see changes happen for us and those around us. As we pray for our pastors to be encouraged in their role in the church, as we beseech God for a supernatural wave of His Holy Spirit to envelope our churches, and as we lift our own personal prayer requests to God, we will see the body of Christ rise up to be the force Jesus has called it to be on this earth.

Now come with us as we start this wonderful journey together.

Part 2: Daily Prayers

Intimacy with God

Jim & Cathy Maxim

"Walking with God down the avenues of prayer we acquire
something of His likeness, and unconsciously we become
witnesses to others of His beauty and His grace."[3]
—E. M. Bounds

*"If anyone loves Me, he will keep My word; and My
Father will love him, and We will come to him and **make
Our home with him**."*
—John 14:23

Jesus Christ spoke these glorious words of promise to His
disciples: To the one who loves Him and follows His teaching,
God the Father, God the Son, and God the Spirit would come
into his heart and make a home in him forever! It is astounding that God Himself would make His home in us. Is there any
greater privilege on this earth than to be in such intimate fellowship with almighty God?

Fellowship with the Father, Son, and Holy Spirit is the
greatest thing we will ever experience. Being in "Their" presence
has no equal. We were made for this purpose. We are the choice
"They" made. We were created in the likeness of God from the
beginning of creation. We are heirs of God and joint heirs with
Jesus Christ. We are agents of heaven enforcing Christ's victory on the earth. We were destined to be in "Their" presence,

---

3. E. M. Bounds, *Purpose in Prayer*, 42.

"walking with God down the avenues of prayer." The end of all we do is echo the anthem of heaven: *"Holy, holy, holy"* (Revelation 4:8). The best news of all is that we don't need to wait until heaven to experience the presence of the Godhead—we can experience it now—in prayer.

I long for that type of closeness with God the Father, God the Son, and God the Holy Spirit. *"We will come to Him and make Our home with him."* I am completely overcome with the privilege that we have in the Lord. That the God of the Universe would want to love us is hard to conceive. That He would want to visit us might be amazing enough, but the triune God is making a home with His people. Like the father of the Prodigal Son, He forgives us, embraces us, and wants us to dwell together under the same roof. That promise is not just for the life to come but for right now. We can fellowship with God in prayer and the reading of His Word.

This is the essence of our first day of prayer: understanding the vital importance of having an intimate relationship with God. For me, there is nothing greater than to feel His love and to know that He is listening to me and enjoying my company as I am enjoying His. I can come to Him and speak with Him, tell Him the burdens on my heart, ask Him to help me or to help someone I am praying for. I wouldn't know what to do if God did not allow me to talk with Him and sense His love and acceptance of me as His son.

What in life could compare with being with God? What could possibly mean as much to us as God Himself touching us with His presence and wanting to be with us? This is the gift of prayer, being allowed to walk with almighty God in His presence and to be with Him. This is truly our first calling.

Brothers and sisters, if you are uncertain of your standing with God, open your heart and mind to Him and bow in His presence. Confess His holiness. Confess your sin to Him, everything once and for all, and then accept the redemption you have received with the death and resurrection of Jesus Christ. Place Him on the throne of your life and humble yourself in His presence. He longs to hold you in His arms and to love you completely. He alone is the Most High God, and He alone is worthy. Worship Him with the words of your mouth; bless Him and bow before Him.

God is calling you into a life of prayer and fellowship with Him. He has given you the privilege of coming to Him. The Father, Son, and Holy Spirit have chosen to make their abode in you. This, my friend, is the greatest privilege the universe will ever know.

In His goodness, God is always—constantly, continually, forever—reaching out to everyone in mankind to have a one-on-one relationship with Him. God longs to reveal Himself to His people because His very nature is love. There is nothing God will not do for His children when they are spiritually in the place where He longs for them to be. Jesus promised us, *"Whatever you ask in My name, that I will do"* (John 14:13).

Take a moment to write down prayer requests you want to lift up before the Lord during these twenty-one days of intercessory prayer.

Prayers for your pastor and his family:

_____

_____

Your church:

_____

_____

Your family:

_____

_____

Your job/finances:

_____

_____

Now join us as we go before the Lord together in prayer by visiting our website: www.acts413.net/21days or www.strategic renewal.com/21days. Pray together with us on Day 1.

Day 2
What Is Prayer?

Jim & Cathy Maxim

"Prayer is the nearest approach to God, and the highest enjoyment of Him, that we are capable of in this life."[4]
—*William Law*

"*Devote yourselves to prayer, being watchful and thankful.*"
—Colossians 4:2 (NIV)

"*Be joyful in hope, patient in affliction, faithful in prayer.*"
—Romans 12:12 (NIV)

Prayer is first and foremost our fellowship with God the Father; Jesus, His Son; and the Holy Spirit. It is an intimate relationship

---

4. William Law, *A Serious Call to a Devout and Holy Life*, 3rd. ed. (London: W. Inny and R. Manby, 1733), 164.

with them in which we can speak from the depths of our heart and hear God's answer to our prayers through the Word and the actions He takes in our lives. Prayer is a blessed communication between you and me and the almighty God of the universe.

Prayer is how God uses time to show us His wonder. Prayer is the activity that God uses to enable His presence to penetrate our consciousness. His presence is the only thing that can literally change any dynamic that exists. His presence contains power that the world cannot understand and power that is reserved only for His redeemed.

Prayer is God saturating our minds, or our thoughts, with His influence. Prayer will control our emotions and permit His truth to bring down the negative forces of darkness that are speaking lies to our minds and trying to corrupt our thoughts.

Prayer is not a natural activity, and the world knows little, if anything at all, about the power associated with our prayers. That is why we will be learning all we can about the power of prayer in our personal lives and the lives of our pastors and churches during these twenty-one days.

Prayer is reserved for you and me. Prayer is the main ingredient in the life of a follower of Jesus Christ. We know that prayer is communication with God the Father through the blood of Jesus Christ and empowered by the Holy Spirit. Prayer is what enables the Holy Spirit to use a man or woman or a church for God's glory. The Holy Spirit will pray through us; He will also pray for us when we are not sure how to pray for any given situation.

In the same way the Spirit also helps our weakness; for we do not know how to pray as we should, but the Spirit Himself intercedes for us with groanings too deep for words; and He

> *who searches the hearts knows what the mind of the Spirit*
> *is, because He intercedes for the saints according to the will*
> *of God.*   (Romans 8:26–27 NASB)

Prayer is the fuel of the Holy Spirit. We get our power from the Holy Spirit, and our "spiritual tank" is filled up through our time with God in prayer. *"But you, beloved, [keep on] building yourselves up on your most holy faith, praying in the Holy Spirit"* (Jude 1:20). Prayer is where we give ourselves to His calling, and it's there that He enables us to accomplish His will in our lives and in the life of the church. I believe that prayer in the church, specifically prayer to encourage and uplift our pastors and leaders in the church, will set the body of Christ on fire for the kingdom of God.

Prayer is true fellowship with God. Prayer is the time God has reserved for us when He can recalibrate our thinking and renew His peace in our mind and soul. Prayer is heaven's funnel for us to be renewed. Prayer is strengthening our connection to the unseen home we have with our Father. Prayer is God's way of saying, "I am yours, and you are Mine; come and talk with Me."

I believe that, through prayer, we will enter into a new dimension in our walk with Him. I believe the destiny God has for us starts to unfold rapidly when we submit our heart and soul to Him for His eternal purposes in our lives, when we accept the awesome privilege of talking with God and receiving from Him the majesty of His presence.

Since prayer is all these things and so much more, please join us as we pray together, in the power and guidance of the Holy Spirit, for ourselves, our loved ones, our pastors, and their families.

Day 3
Jesus Prayed

Jim & Cathy Maxim

"You can do more than pray after you have prayed…but
you cannot do more than pray until you have prayed."[5]
—A. J. Gordon

*"One of His disciples said to Him,
'Lord, teach us to pray.'"*
—Luke 11:1

Prayer was the single most important ritual in Jesus's life. Prayer was the single most important time in Jesus's life. Writing this twice was not a misprint—it is that important for us to understand! Jesus spent long nights in prayer to His heavenly Father so that He could move in His Father's will and power. Prayer was the greatest tool Jesus used to change the lives of others.

We have to understand this! Jesus spent hours communicating with His Father in prayer so that He could accomplish the Father's will every single day. *"One of those days Jesus went out to a mountainside to pray, and spent the night praying to God"* (Luke 6:12 NIV). After His prayer times, Jesus could say, "I only do the things I see my Father doing." (See John 5:19.) Jesus could reach through the darkness to rescue the lost and hurting because His Father shared the power and plan with Him through prayer.

Jesus knew the value of meeting with His Father first and foremost every day and in everything He did. The very essence

---

5. A. J. Gordon quoted in E. M. Bounds, *Purpose in Prayer*, 20.

of His life was bathed in constant communication with His Father. Jesus accomplished more in less time and with greater lasting value than anyone else who ever walked the earth. The disciples saw this up close and personal as they watched Him and knew that His source of power to fulfill His destiny was directly related to His time with the Father. So the disciples asked Him, *"Lord, teach us to pray."* You know His response—a prayer recognizing the glory of the Father and our need for Him in every instance of our lives.

> *Our Father which art in heaven, hallowed be thy name. Thy kingdom come, thy will be done in earth, as it is in heaven. Give us this day our daily bread. And forgive us our debts, as we forgive our debtors. And lead us not into temptation, but deliver us from evil: for thine is the kingdom, and the power, and the glory, for ever. Amen.*
>
> (Matthew 6:9–13 KJV)

Jesus is the perfect model of prayer for us:

> *Therefore I tell you, whatever you ask for in prayer, believe that you have received it, and it will be yours. And when you stand praying, if you hold anything against anyone, forgive him, so that your Father in heaven may forgive you your sins.*
>
> (Mark 11:24–25 NIV)

> *Truly, truly, I say to you, whoever believes in me will also do the works that I do; and greater things than these will he do, because I am going to the Father. **Whatever you ask in my name, this I will do, that the Father may be glorified in***

the Son. If you ask me anything in my name, I will do it.
(John 14:12–14 ESV)

Very early in the morning, while it was still dark, Jesus got up, left the house and went off to a solitary place, where he prayed."
(Mark 1:35 NIV)

In the end, prayer was the time Jesus spent in close communication with God the Father. Through that time of fellowship, Jesus was given both the knowledge and the power to do what His Father wanted Him to do on the earth. To forgive, to heal, to comfort, to feed, to set free—Jesus accomplished all these things as a result of His time of prayer.

Learn to pray the way Jesus prayed for the concerns in your life, for the power of God to move through your church, and for the encouragement and strength of your pastor as he seeks to lead the flock. Say to the Lord yourself, "Teach me to pray." And He will.

Join us at www.acts413.net/21days or www.strategic renewal.com/21days to come before God's throne together.

Day 4
I Love the Lord

Cathy Maxim

"You can always give without loving,
but you can never love without giving."
—*Amy Carmichael*

> *"I love the LORD because he hears my voice and my prayer*
> *for mercy. Because he bends down to listen,*
> *I will pray as long as I have breath!"*
> —Psalm 116:1–2 (NLT)

Another version says, *"Because **He** has inclined His ear to me, therefore I shall call upon **Him** as long as I live"* (Psalm 116:2 NASB), but I love the picture of a Father bending down to hear his child. How many times have you stooped down to look a child in the face to speak to him or her? We do this because we want them to focus on us or want them to know we are listening to them. We want them to feel and know they are important!

The words in these two verses paint that picture to me. They go deep into my heart and bring healing! I am a child of God. I am important to Him. The Lord wants to hear my needs and requests. He wants to be a part of my life, and I need Him to be my life. I need His life flowing down to me, flowing in me, and flooding my mind, body, and spirit. I need this because I need healing every day.

My mind, body, and spirit are attacked every day. Life crowds in and tries to steal my intimacy with God. Busyness leaves us rushing through the day, failing to see those around us, failing to see the needs around us. When we don't have new strength from the Lord every morning, we don't want to look and see the needs of others. We can't! The burden is too great, so we just walk on by.

There is only one way off this merry-go-round, and that is prayer! Time with Him. *"I love the LORD because he hears my voice and prayer for mercy"*! He hears. He has given me this one life to live. He knows all the people in my life. He knows all the needs of their lives. And He has asked me to care, to intercede for them, to stand in the gap for them, to be a bridge for them to heaven, to stand with them in their fight! *"When the enemy comes in like a flood, the Spirit of the LORD will lift up a standard against him"* (Isaiah 59:19). We need the Spirit of God to flow through us like floodwater to make our enemies flee!

Isaiah paints a picture of victory to me. It's the kind of victory I try to apply to my prayer life. I want to see healing in people's lives. I want to believe for a job situation to be handled or for a prodigal son or daughter to come home to Jesus:

> *Behold, I will lift up my hand to the nations, and raise my signal to the peoples; and they shall bring your sons in their arms, and your daughters shall be carried on their shoulders. Kings shall be your foster fathers, and their queens your nursing mothers. With their faces to the ground they shall bow down to you, and lick the dust of your feet. Then you will know that I am the LORD; those who wait for me shall not be put to shame.* (Isaiah 49:22–23 ESV)

Begin to see your prayers as the standard, the banner that proclaims, "In the name of Jesus, this siege ends here and now!" Then wait and praise Him; then wait some more and praise Him. We are calling the armies of heaven to fight with us, to do what we cannot do. We are believing our Father who bends down low, who hears our voice and prayers for mercy!

Join us in prayer today as we go before the loving Father who bends down from heaven to hear our cry. We will pray in faith together that the One who hears our prayers will answer us. Join us for prayer on Day 4 by visiting www.acts413.net/21days or www.strategicrenewal.com/21days.

Day 5

Pray That I Speak Fearlessly

Jim & Cathy Maxim

"No learning can make up for the failure to pray.
No earnestness, no diligence, no study,
no gifts will supply its lack."[6]
—E. M. Bounds

*"Pray in the Spirit on all occasions with all kinds of prayers
and requests. With this in mind, be alert and always keep
on praying for all the Lord's people.* **Pray also for me,** *that
whenever I speak, words may be given me so that I will
fearlessly make known the mystery of the gospel, for which
I am an ambassador in chains.* **Pray that I may declare it
fearlessly, as I should."**
—Ephesians 6:18–20 (NIV)

Paul was a firebrand leader in the early church. He faced angry mobs of Jewish leaders and idol worshipers while proclaiming the gospel message of Jesus Christ. His letters to the churches throughout the Middle East have provided many foundational teachings for the church. Yet Paul asked his brothers and sisters in Christ to pray for him. Why?

The apostle Paul had studied for years, yet he knew that he could never accomplish God's call on his life in his own wisdom. As E. M. Bounds said, nothing can make up for a lack of prayer, not even years of study and the natural gifts that Paul had been

---

6. E. M. Bounds, *Power Through Prayer* (Morrisville, NC: Lulu Press, 2013).

given. The apostle knew he had to rely on the supernatural power of the Holy Spirit for strength and guidance to complete his task. Paul needed the encouragement of his brothers and sisters lifting him up in prayer before the God of heaven.

In Ephesians, chapter 6, Paul asked the church to pray specifically that he would "*fearlessly*" declare the message of salvation in Jesus Christ in every situation. "*Pray also for me, that whenever I speak, words may be given me so that I will fearlessly make known the mystery of the gospel*" (verse 19). Did that mean that Paul was afraid? That he was not up to the task? I believe it meant that Paul was human—just as every leader in the church today is human—and that he needed the fervent prayers of fellow believers to lift him up and encourage him in his calling. Jesus Himself, the Son of God, asked Peter, James, and John to pray with Him in the garden of Gethsemane that He would have the strength to complete God's plan of redemption.

Just like in Paul's case, only God can supply us with the strength we need to serve Him. Many times, with good intentions, those in ministry (lay leaders included) allow themselves to get drained to the point of total exhaustion, so that the ministry seems like too much for them to continue. Through the power of the Holy Spirit, God promises to renew our strength like the eagle (see Isaiah 40:31), but sometimes, that just seems too good to be true or too far out of reach. That is why we have a heart for these twenty-one days of corporate intercession; we feel called by God to walk through this time of prayer renewal for pastors, leaders, and the body of Christ, that His power may move through everyone who has joined us on the journey of praying together.

God is doing something mighty in His people in the church today, and the opposition to God's work will only get stronger.

So will God's holy presence, as we seek Him in prayer and confess His holiness and His power upon our families and the ministry staff of our churches, who serve Him on our behalf.

Please join us in the prayer of agreement today as God moves in strength and power in our midst. Visit www.acts413.net/21days or www.strategicrenewal.com/21days.

Day 6
For the Sake of the Gospel

Daniel Henderson

"We spend more prayer energy trying to
keep sick Christians out of heaven than trying to keep
lost people out of hell."
—*James Walker*

*"At the same time, pray also for us, that God may open to
us a door for the word, to declare the mystery of Christ, on
account of which I am in prison—that I may make it clear,
which is how I ought to speak."*
—Colossians 4:3–4 (ESV)

Asking is a vital component of our relationship with God. This is true because He has commanded us to seek Him as our ultimate source in all things. He has ordained prayer as the means by which we depend on and trust in Him. He answers our prayers to give us what He knows we need to bring Him glory.

In today's devotional, I want to shift things from praying for ourselves to praying the gospel itself. We have to admit that, in today's culture, permanently infected with materialism and a consumer mind-set, it is sometimes difficult for Christians to ask for things from God without a fundamentally selfish reason or a chronic aversion to suffering in any form. Too often, we pray to escape our difficulties rather to embrace discipleship in Christ.

Like many others, I love it when God answers my prayers in ways that make my life more pleasant or pain free. However, I am learning that my deepest needs are met when my heart is most closely aligned with the Word of God, the Son of God, the Spirit of God, and the purposes of God. I feel God calling me and many others I know beyond superficial solutions as the focus of our prayers. Asking is the doorway, not just to getting our next lunch or luxury item, but also to discovering the profound joy of a transformed life in Christ.

I am so grateful the Father cares about every detail of my life. He even counts the hairs on my head (see Luke 12:7), which does not take as long for me as it does for the average person! But it is so easy to reduce our focus in prayer to the typical "organ recital" concerns about Paula's pimples, Billy's bile duct, Sarah's stomach ache, and Artie's appendix. Our Father knows, cares, and is fully capable of taking care of all these needs according to His will and glory, but the privilege of prayer offers so much more.

We know we are supposed to bring our requests to God, but one of the most important questions we need to ask is, "How does the content of our prayers differ from the biblical patterns and teaching about the things we should be praying about?" The prayer requests we find in the Bible seem dramatically shorter, deeper, and fundamentally different in nature than the lists that tend to dominate the prayers of modern Christians.

Scripture records numerous examples of Jesus's prayer life. We find six references to Jesus's prayers that give no clear indication of the content. (See Mark 1:35; 6:46; Luke 3:21; 9:18, 28; 11:1.) We find He often withdrew from activity to enjoy private communion with the Father. While we do not know the substance of His prayers in these times, it appears they were directly related to fresh empowerment for His selfless, sacrificial service. There were also occasions when Jesus blessed people, but His exact words were not provided. (See Mark 10:16; Luke 24:50.)

We do find other brief accounts of the content of Jesus's prayers and the themes that shaped His spoken prayers. (See Matthew 11:25; 26:39, 42; 27:46; Mark 14:36; 15:34; Luke 22:31–32, 42; 23:34, 46; John 11:41–42; 12:27–28; 17.) If you review all of these, you will find that Jesus always prayed for the glory of the Father and was in complete submission to His will. His prayers always focused on His mission and the fruitful mission of His followers.

We also see the early church in prayer, most often seeking the advancement of the gospel in virtually every situation. They prayed daily as part of a vital regimen of spiritual growth—for the sake of the gospel. (See Acts 2:42.) In the face of attack, they gathered to pray from the Scriptures, requesting fresh power for boldness—for the sake of the gospel. (See Acts 4:31.) When they were persecuted, they rejoiced in God for the honor of suffering rather than asking for a reprieve—for the sake of the gospel. (See Acts 5:41.) When Peter was in jail, they prayed for his release—for the sake of the gospel. (See Acts 12:5.) When Paul and Silas were in jail, they rejoiced in prayer and trusted God in singing—for the sake of the gospel. (See Acts 16:25.)

Of course, we know how Paul prayed because we have the account of his prayers in the New Testament. (See Ephesians 1:3–23; 3:14–21; Philippians 1:3–11; Colossians 1:3–14; 1 Thessalonians 3:9–13; 2 Thessalonians 1:3–12.) With close observation, it becomes clear that every one of Paul's model prayers spring from expressions of thanksgiving, truths about God, and notes of praise. They are the fruit of his worship and intimate, experiential knowledge of the person of Christ.

Have you noticed the focus of Paul's prayer request at the beginning of this devotional? He prayed that doors would be opened to share the Word of God and *"the mystery of Christ"* (Colossians 4:3). It represents his regular focus in prayer. (See Acts 20:23–24; Romans 15:30–33; 2 Corinthians 1:9–11; Ephesians 6:19; Philippians 1:19–20; Colossians 4:3–4; 1 Thessalonians 5:25; 2 Thessalonians 3:1.) All of Paul's prayer requests focused on his desire to accomplish his mission by boldly and enduringly proclaiming the gospel so that Christ might be magnified in and through him—in life or in death.

Perhaps the fundamental difference between our prayer lists and the prayer concerns we find in the Bible is that we pray about personal problems, while most of the biblical prayers focused on Christ's purposes. Worship-based prayers set the foundation for something other than "me" prayers, because they start with "Thee." This changes the nature of how we pray. We need to continually learn from the Father how we should pray.

Dr. D. A. Carson, in his outstanding book *A Call to Spiritual Reformation: Priorities from Paul and His Prayers*, presented a powerful inquiry that should motivate us to evaluate the nature of our prayer lists. He wrote,

We must ask ourselves how far the petitions we commonly present to God are in line with what Paul prays for. Suppose, for example, that 80 or 90 percent of our petitions ask God for good health, recovery from illness, safety on the road, a good job, success in exams, the emotional needs of our children, success in our mortgage application, and much more of the same. How much of Paul's praying revolves around equivalent items? If the center of our praying is far removed from the center of Paul's praying, then even our very praying may serve as a wretched testimony to the remarkable success of the processes of paganization in our life and thought.[7]

Strong words indeed! Yet they are a necessary wake-up call as we look at the values, aspirations, and longings that drive our prayers.

Lord, please teach us to pray as Jesus did, as the early church did, and as Paul did. Teach us to lift our focus of prayer to Your purposes and plans both for ourselves and for our leaders. Join us for prayer on Day 6 at www.acts413.net/21days or www.strategic renewal.com/21days.

Day 7
The Secret Closet

Jim Maxim

"Therefore, whether the desire for prayer is on you or not,
get to your closet at the set time; shut yourself in with

---

7. D. A. Carson, *A Call to Spiritual Reformation: Priorities from Paul and His Prayers* (Grand Rapids, MI: Baker Academic, 1992), 96–97.

God; wait upon Him; seek His face; realize Him; pray."[8]
—R. F. Horton

"But you, when you pray, go into your inner room [closet],
close your door and pray to your Father who is in secret,
and your Father who sees what is done in secret will
reward you."
—Matthew 6:6 (NASB)

I am in Las Vegas at a business convention, and it is 3:20 a.m. God, the Holy Spirit, has stirred me to get out of bed and spend time with Him. The only reason I am giving you a glimpse of my relationship with Him is because of the quote He wants me to share with you today. "Get into your closet at the set time."

What is your closet? Your closet is that place where you can be alone with God to share whatever is on your heart and to listen for His voice speaking through the Bible or in your spirit. The set time is whenever He speaks with you and stirs you to come away with Him into your prayer closet and close the door. Most days, He comes into my room around 5 a.m.—some days earlier—but mostly between 4 and 5 a.m., and He wakes me up because He wants to spend time with me. How can I say "no" to Him? It's been decades now of this intimacy with God, and most days, I need no alarm clock.

At first, I had been ignorant of God's stirring and just thought I needed to roll over and try my other side to go back to sleep. When He didn't leave me alone, I realized that my Father was there desiring to spend time with me. Oh, what a blessing! Oh, what a thrill! He really wanted to spend time with me alone in my

---

8. R. F. Horton quoted in Tim Clinton and Max Davis, *Ignite Your Faith: Get Back in the Fight* (Shippensburg, PA: Destiny Image Publishers, 2014).

secret place. Remember Jesus said, *"When you pray, go into your inner room, close the door and pray…and your Father who sees what is done in secret will reward you"* (Matthew 6:6 NASB). Each of us has a secret place to meet with God, and it's there that God unfolds our own hearts to us. God gently draws us closer to Himself.

In the end, I am real with God during prayer in the secret closet, and I am in a position to really hear from Him. This intimate prayer is what Jesus longs for us to experience. This prayer brings us into the place where our soul is touching the heart of God.

Jeremiah said God longs to show us secret, hidden things: *"Call to Me, and I will answer you, and show you great and mighty things, which you do not know"* (Jeremiah 33:3). Isaiah 45:3 (ESV) says, *"I will give you the treasures of darkness and the hoards in secret places, that you may know that it is I, the LORD."*

Think about this for a few minutes with me: God, the Creator of the entire universe, mankind, the animals, the planets, the millions of light years, and the expanse of the heaven, wants to come to me and fellowship in the inner room, in a secret place that just includes the two of us. He really wants a close communion with me. He wants me to be His friend!

God wants you to be His friend, too, and He wants to be your friend! Say this out loud: "God wants me to be His friend, and He wants to be my friend." Jesus wanted us to be certain of this: *"No longer do I call you servants, for the servant does not know what his master is doing; but I have called you friends, for all that I have heard from my Father I have made known to you"* (John 15:15 ESV).

It's a two-way friendship. God does not want a one-way relationship in which He pursues you and you continue to stiff-arm

Him. He wants you to understand that you can have as much of Him as you want! The pursuit of your heavenly Father is initiated by Him, revealed in Jesus, and sustained by His Holy Spirit, but it requires that you participate in this relationship.

You need to show up! You need to set apart a time to meet with the Lord daily. Why God wants to spend time with us is something that can be explained only by the unconditional love He shows us in His Word, but He promises that if we spend time in prayer in the secret place, He will reward us openly. That is a promise that will change lives for eternity!

Powerful things happen in the secret place. In your conversation with the God who loves you today, lift up your pastor and the leaders of your church, that they would find God's presence and power in their time alone with Him. Lift up your family members and friends who need the Lord to touch their lives today. Let's set a time for our own daily appointment with God in the secret place, where hearts are changed forever.

Join us now for prayer at www.acts413.net/21days or www.strategicrenewal.com/21days. God hears and answers the prayers of His people!

Day 8
Earnest Prayer for Him

Jim & Cathy Maxim

"Men may spurn our appeals, reject our message,
oppose our arguments, despise our persons, but they

are helpless against our prayers."[9]
—*J. Sidlow Baxter*

*"About that time Herod the king laid violent hands on some
who belonged to the church. He killed James the brother of
John with the sword, and when he saw that it pleased the
Jews, he proceeded to arrest Peter also. This was during the
days of Unleavened Bread. And when he had seized him,
he put him in prison, delivering him over to four squads of
soldiers to guard him, intending after the Passover to bring
him out to the people. So Peter was kept in prison, **but
earnest prayer for him was made to God by the church**."*
—Acts 12:1–5 (ESV)

Let's take a close look at the real meaning of the bolded words:

But: "Oh, no, you don't!" the church said. "He's our brother,
and you can't have him!"

Earnest: An intense, dedicated, focused, desperate, physically exhausting, committed to achieving the desired goal, "no
quitting in me because of Him in me" kind of prayer.

Prayer: God's method given to the church to permit us to partner with the divine Creator to accomplish His goals in the earth.

To God: The sovereign Ruler of the entire universe—the
King, the Lord, our Father.

By the church: believers in Christ, united in prayers of
agreement.

Earnest prayer to God—it's mountain-moving kind of
prayer!

---

9. J. Sidlow Baxter quoted in William Carr Walter and Walter L. Larimore,
Going Public with Your Faith: Becoming a Spiritual Influence at Work (Grand
Rapids, MI: Zondervan, 2003), 193.

So what happened when the early church prayed? God sent an angel to Peter in the middle of the night, woke him up, released him from his chains, and led him right out of prison to where the church was praying for him! Peter thought it was a dream. When he realized that it was very real, *"he went to the house of Mary, the mother of John whose other name was Mark, where many were gathered together and were praying"* (Acts 12:12 ESV).

Peter could thank God for people who understood the value of "earnest prayer." The church was working in the spirit realm so that God would work in the supernatural realm. *"But earnest prayer for him was made to God by the church"* (Acts 12:5 ESV)!

I am not saying that every time we pray, we get instant miracles like this. I am saying that we can receive tremendous encouragement and hope when we realize that the activity of prayer is sacred to God—so much so that He holds our prayers in a bowl in heaven (see Revelation 5:8), and our prayers are eternal.

I am so grateful that my mother, Isobel Maxim, would not let me go. For years, she made earnest prayer to God for me when I was deeply lost, and God set me free. Although it was not instantaneous, nevertheless, in His perfect timing, the day came. And because of the earnest prayer she made for me, my life in Christ—my relationship with God Almighty, my wife, my children, my grandchildren, my fellowship in the body of Christ, my work—all has been possible.

Jesus said,

> *Have faith in God. Truly, I say to you, whoever says to this mountain, 'Be taken up and thrown into the sea,' and does not doubt in his heart, but believes that what he says will come to pass, it will be done for him. Therefore I tell you,*

whatever you ask in prayer, believe that you have received it, and it will be yours."　　　　　(Mark 11:22–24 ESV)

This doesn't mean it will be in your time, but Jesus did say it will be yours: *"Without faith it is impossible to please [God], for he who comes to God must believe that He is, and that He is a rewarder of those **who diligently seek Him**"* (Hebrews 11:6).

Let's take God at His Word! Let's go before God the Father and bring earnest, diligent prayers, first for the pastors of our churches, as we pledge to pray for them during these twenty-one days. Then, let's pray earnestly for loved ones who may be far from God, petitioning Him for their release from the prison that holds them in bondage.

I don't ever want to be lighthearted or casual in my requests to God, do you? He has promised to reward those who diligently seek Him!

Join us as we pray earnestly together, bringing our requests before a loving and attentive God. Visit www.acts413.net/21days or www.strategicrenewal.com/21days.

Day 9
Prayer Is Our Weapon

Jim & Cathy Maxim

"Prayer is **our most formidable weapon**, but the one in which we are the least skilled, the most adverse to its use."[10]
—E. M. Bounds

---

10. E. M. Bounds, *Purpose in Prayer*, 48.

*"The weapons of our warfare are not natural, manmade, or carnal, but Divine weapons for **the pulling down of strongholds.** And we use these weapons against anything lifted up against the name of God, **and we bring every negative thought captive to the obedience of Christ.**"*
—2 Corinthians 10:4–5

Just what does Paul mean by *"the weapons of our warfare"*? He is speaking of mighty spiritual weapons—not of men, but of God—that can set us free from the enemy's strongholds over our lives. Weapons like prayer, faith, and the Word of God.

Have you ever considered prayer as a weapon? It seems from this Scripture that Paul is admonishing us to be on the offense as we use our spiritual weapons to pull down strongholds in our lives and in the lives of those we love!

A stronghold is a place that has been fortified to protect it against attack, such as a fort or fortress. What kind of strongholds is Paul talking about? Any thought, plan, or action that rises up against the knowledge of God. Paul declared that we have spiritual weapons from God Almighty that will pull down these strongholds and will enable us to "capture every negative thought and bring it into submission to the obedience of Christ." (See 2 Corinthians 10:5.)

In other words, if we or someone we love believe the negative lies of the enemy instead of the Word of God—if we are enslaved by Satan's lies that say we are not good enough, we don't belong to God, we will fail at everything we attempt in life, we need drugs or alcohol to make it through a day—we must pull down these strongholds with the spiritual weapons that God has provided. If what we are seeing and dwelling on, or if what is happening to us, is contrary to God's Word, then God has equipped us with the weapons of prayer, faith, and the Word of God to use against those things so that they do not have any influence over our thoughts and our lives!

Remember the day you first saw the truth about Jesus? Remember the day it all became clear to you that He had paid the price to set you free? Remember the day the "strongholds" in your life came tumbling down and you were no longer held captive to the lies Satan had designed for you? Remember when the fortress was destroyed because someone prayed for you using his or her weapon to accomplish God's purpose in your life, which is to know Him and to love Him?

Let's be practical here. If we have a loved one caught up in an addiction, how are we to use these spiritual weapons to address it as Christians? Use prayer as a spiritual weapon in their lives. God has said that our weapons are mighty to pull down strongholds in our loved one's life. (See 2 Corinthians 10:4.) As we earnestly pray for them, we can bring down the demonic strongholds that hinder them from seeing the truth of God's love. Our intercession over them causes the demonic forces to lose their grip so that our loved ones may see the deception Satan has played upon them. Our prayers will bring them the truth. Remember Jesus's words *"You shall know the truth, and the truth shall make you free"* (John 8:32).

It might seem strange that prayer has the power to destroy these strongholds and change a person's life for eternity. However, we have to think with a heavenly perspective. Prayer is communication with God that operates on the rules and laws of the spiritual world. We cannot fight our spiritual battles by human means! We must use the spiritual weapons that God offers to us—and, as E. M. Bounds has said, prayer is the most formidable weapon of all.

In prayer to an almighty God, we can "bind the enemy" (see Matthew 16:19) on other people's behalf and bring all their thoughts into captivity to God's Word. As we pray for God to intervene in their lives, they will begin to see that God is reaching out to them in love. Your prayers become a catalyst that is mobilizing the power of God on their behalf! Prayer is the power that God gave His church, and we must use it. Prayer is what will set them free!

Can you see how prayer was designed by God as the true weapon of the church to enforce His purposes on the earth? Can you see that being "prayed up" and ready for battle is a privilege? Do you believe that, if you set your face to prayer, God Himself will meet you? The presence of God, the actual presence of God, will cause you to flow in the power of the Holy Spirit.

Prayer is God's weapon to the church that gives us the power to knock down and destroy the strongholds that come against the hearts and minds of our pastors and their families. Satan's attempt to discourage them and to thwart their ministry can seem like a fortress they cannot overcome. In intercessory prayer, God has given us the power to pray on their behalf, destroying all attacks of the enemy!

Join us today in prayer that the weapons of our warfare will be mighty for the pulling down of strongholds in our lives and the lives of those around us. Tune into the Day 9 prayer time at www.acts413.net/21days or www.strategicrenewal.com/21days.

Day 10
A Deeper Foundation

Jim Maxim

"You can only go as far
for God as you have time with God."
—Jim Maxim

*"He is like a man building a house, who dug deep and laid
the foundation on the rock. And when a flood arose, the
stream broke against that house and could not shake it,
because it had been well built."*
—Luke 6:48 (ESV)

I was in downtown Pittsburgh one afternoon sitting at a red light and, as I looked over to my left, I saw a large construction site being developed. The men were wearing their work belts, carrying different pieces of building materials, and very intently focusing on getting their jobs done. The architects had their drawings spread out as they reviewed plans with the foreman. The cement trucks were all lined up on the street ready to pour the foundation. I was wondering where they were going to start pouring when I saw it—a giant hole.

I wondered how deep it was. I sat up in my seat as tall as I could to see the bottom of the hole. I was amazed at how far down it went. At that moment, I felt the Holy Spirit gently moving in my heart and speaking softly to me: *Jim, you can go with God only as far as you have time with God. The greater the size of the building, the deeper its foundation must be.* Immediately, I understood what He was saying. I could see my life in front of me; I could see the desire Cathy and I had to walk with God, to bring Him glory, and to build His church in whatever way He chose with us. He was gently reminding me that the higher we desired to build in His name, the deeper we had to go in our relationship with Him.

I thought of all the Christian men and women of God I had read about, those who were used by God generations ago and those being used by Him today to build His kingdom. I could see the one common denominator: unlike so many others, they understood that their first priority was to be with Him.

"You can go with God only as far as you have time with Him. There are no shortcuts for anyone and there never will be." Our spirit man, the real us, must be in God's presence continually, because that's where we are fed and watered. There we minister to Him and He changes us. Remember, the very first thing God our Father did after accepting the sacrifice of Jesus on the cross was to tear the veil that separated mankind from walking into the Holy of Holies. Before that day, only the high priest could enter God's presence. Now it is open to everyone who believes in the Lord Jesus Christ and is saved. Our greatest privilege is to be with God.

I knew that God was waiting for me to discipline myself to spend more time with Him. I knew that His desire was to show me more of Himself and the true power of prayer. I knew that He was offering me what He has for all His children, a deeper life with Him. He was waiting for my response. It wasn't long after this that God's blessing exploded in so many areas of our lives. It was as if this secret, "the secret place," was no longer a secret to us. Prayer had become the reality God had intended all along.

*Therefore, confess your sins to one another, and pray for one another so that you may be healed. **The effective prayer of*** *a righteous man can accomplish much."*

(James 5:16 NASB)

Each of us must come to the realization that we can accomplish much more in every area of our lives when our attitude and actions about prayer are "effective and fervent." (See James 5:16 KJV.) God delights in answering those fervent prayers, but most of us in every walk of life have believed the enemy's lie that we are "too busy" for time alone with God.

Today, we will come to the Lord in prayer to take that lie *"captive to the obedience of Christ"* (2 Corinthians 10:5). No one is too busy to come before God in the quiet of the secret place. We will pray for our pastors and our church leaders as well, that they would spend time alone with God no matter how hectic their lives might be. We will pray that the church will come together to pray for the pastors' burdens as they seek God's face for the congregation. And we will pray for one another, that we may remember that "you can go with God only as far as you have time with God."

Join us today for prayer on Day 10 at www.acts413.net/ 21days or www.strategicrenewal.com/21days.

Day 11
Discipline in Prayer Brings Peace

Jim & Cathy Maxim

"The battle of prayer is against two things: wandering thoughts and lack of intimacy with God's character as revealed in His Word. Neither can be cured at once,

but they can be cured by discipline."[11]
—*Oswald Chambers*

*"You will keep him in perfect peace, whose mind is stayed
on You, because he trusts in You."*
—Isaiah 26:3

The discipline of prayer will change every aspect of your life for the better. God said that He would keep in perfect peace whoever keeps his mind on Him. Perfect peace—what would the world pay to have perfect peace?

My dear brothers and sisters, this is our eleventh day of seeking God together. Perhaps you have decided that the world will not dictate your peace, for your peace comes from God and God alone. Are you convinced that your peace is His peace living inside of you?

Nothing that happens to you can ever take this peace. God Himself promised you that if you keep your mind on Him, He will personally keep you in perfect peace. He didn't say the waters of life would never rage or that all hell wouldn't come against you. He said that He would keep in perfect peace whoever keeps his mind on Him.

During our twenty-one days of prayer, perhaps you have decided to discipline yourself and get alone with God the Father, the Lord Jesus, and the Holy Spirit so that you can receive this promise of peace. The decisions you make daily to discipline yourself in prayer, along with the reading of God's Word, are the greatest activities you will ever do! This is when you will

---

11. Oswald Chambers, *Christian Disciplines: Building Strong Character*
(Grand Rapids, MI: Discover House Publishers, 2013).

experience His presence and He will personally place His peace upon you and flowing through you.

Let's look at the Scripture for today one more time: *"You will keep him in perfect peace, whose mind is stayed on You, because he trusts in You."* The promise is not for the person who thinks about God once in a while, but the one who constantly has God in his thoughts.

"Keep" means to have or retain possession of and to continue or cause to continue in a specified condition, position, or course. Synonyms include to remain, to continue to be, to stay, or to carry on.

Jesus came bringing a promise of peace: *"Peace I leave with you, My peace I give to you; not as the world gives do I give to you. Let not your heart be troubled, neither let it be afraid"* (John 14:27).

Jesus also said, *"The thief [devil] comes only to steal and kill and destroy"* (John 10:10 ESV). Our discipline in prayer keeps the devil from stealing our peace. Prayer is the method, the activity, the manner in which we keep on receiving the peace of almighty God, and this is the main reason why prayer is the greatest activity we will ever do!

Satan will go to any length to stop you from spending time alone with God. He knows that you receive your peace when you are alone with the Lord. A Christian living in God's peace is the most dangerous supernatural force alive on the earth. A Christian walking with the power of God's peace upon him or her can accomplish great things for the glory of God. You can become the person God has always intended for you to be. You can actually walk in your God-given destiny. You can be in lockstep with the Holy Spirit. You can keep on being used by Him for His glory.

This daily discipline you have chosen, this activity of prayer, keeps your mind on the things of God and will make you the kind of person whom God can use to pour His love and power on a lost and dying world. And you can watch Him transform your hurting loved ones into people who will love, honor, and serve God alongside of you.

Through the discipline of prayer, you can be used powerfully in the body of Christ to encourage and pray for those in need in your home, in your neighborhood, and in the church. During these days of prayer, and long afterward, your daily prayers can also encourage and build up the pastors in your community as they stand at the forefront of the battle against the enemy and seek God's will for the people in their care.

Let's thank God for His peace that rules and reigns in our hearts, and for the discipline of prayer that enables us to see the miracle of answered prayer in the world around us! Please join us in prayer on Day 11 at www.acts413.net/21days or www.strategic renewal.com/21days.

Day 12
Praying with an Open Bible

Daniel Henderson

"Just as God's Word must reform our theology, our ethics, and our practices, so also must it reform our praying."[12]
—*D. A. Carson*

---

12. D. A. Carson, *A Call to Spiritual Reformation: Priorities from Paul and His Prayers* (Grand Rapids, MI: Baker Book House Company, 1992), 17.

> *"When they were released, they went to their friends and*
> *reported what the chief priests and the elders had said*
> *to them. And when they heard it, they lifted their voices*
> *together to God and said, 'Sovereign Lord, who made the*
> *heaven and the earth and the sea and everything in them,*
> *who through the mouth of our father David, your servant,*
> *said by the Holy Spirit, "Why did the Gentiles rage, and*
> *the peoples plot in vain?"'"*
>
> —Acts 4:23–25 (esv)

Have you ever wondered what a prayer meeting in the early church might have looked like? Although we know that the early Christ followers prayed much and often, we do not have a detailed account of the actual content of their prayers, except in Acts 4:23–31 (a portion of which is featured above). Take a minute to read the entire account carefully and prayerfully, then consider where the early Christians started their prayers and how this guided the focus of their prayers.

You will notice that this paramount example of prayer started with the worship of God as the sovereign Creator, based on the Word of God. They began with their persecution by praying Scripture from the Old Testament (in this case, Psalm 2).

Have you ever noticed that the one who starts a conversation tends to guide the conversation? So, in prayer, how much better it is to let God start the conversation from His Word so that He can guide the conversation based on His living, powerful, and unchanging truth.

Clearly, this is the idea of a truth-based intimacy that shapes our prayers and forms the proper expression of our needs. Again, prayer is not a casual recitation of whatever pains and problems pop into our minds on any given occasion. It is the overflow of a heart focused on the conscious presence of Christ, clinging to Him and to His Word as the source and scope of our lives.

These early church leaders had taken to heart Jesus's words as He taught in the upper room just days before His death: *"If you abide in me, and my words abide in you, ask whatever you wish, and it will be done for you. By this my Father is glorified, that you bear much fruit and so prove to be my disciples"* (John 15:7–8 ESV). Jesus had been teaching them about a life of abiding and bearing fruit, more fruit and much fruit. Now He said that powerful prayer and a life of fruitfulness would come from His Word abiding in them.

Pastor John Piper gave the right perspective when he said,

> There are dozens of instances in the Bible of people praying for desires as natural as the desire for protection from enemies and escape from danger and success in vocation and fertility in marriage, recovery from sickness, etc. My point is not that those desires are wrong. My point is that they should always be subordinate to spiritual desires; kingdom desires; fruit-bearing desires; gospel-spreading, God-centered desires; Christ-exalting, God-glorifying desires. And when our natural desires are felt as a means to these greater desires, then they become the proper subject of prayer."[13]

While it was not always this way, all my praying in the last two decades, both personal and in community, have begun with an open Bible. On a personal level, I read the Scriptures using a

---

13. John Piper, "Ask Whatever You Wish," *Desiring God Ministries* (10 January 1993), https://www.desiringgod.org/messages/ask-whatever-you-wish.

Bible program on my laptop. As specific passages speak to me, I paste them into my journal program. Then, I take time to allow those Bible segments to speak deeply to my heart, and write out my prayers in response. This sense of Christ's presence and the substance of His Word guides my praying for that day. When I miss a day of this kind of praying, which is more often than I wish, I feel the difference and the distance.

George Müller, a renowned man of faith and evangelist who cared for thousands of orphans and established dozens of Christian schools in the 1800s, spoke about the vital role of Scripture in his prayer life. He noted that for years, he tried to pray without starting in the Bible in the morning. Inevitably, his mind wandered for ten, fifteen, even thirty minutes.[14] Then, when he began to start each morning with the Bible to nourish his soul, he found his heart being transformed by the truth, resulting in spontaneous prayers of confession, thanksgiving, intercession, and supplication. This became his daily experience for decades, resulting in great personal growth and power for life and ministry.

Speaking about this very idea, Pastor John Piper noted, "I have seen…that those whose prayers are most saturated with Scripture are generally most fervent and most effective in prayer. And where the mind isn't brimming with the Bible, the heart is not generally brimming with prayer."[15]

So, let us always seek to pray on behalf of our walk with Christ, our families, and our church leaders from a place of

---

14. George Müller, *Autobiography of George Müller* (New Kensington, PA: Whitaker House, 1985), 137–138.
15. John Piper, "How to Pray for a Desolate Church," *Desiring God Ministries* (5 January 1992), https://www.desiringgod.org/messages/how-to-pray-for-a-desolate-church.

abiding in Him and allowing His Word to saturate our minds and guide our words. Then our prayers will not simply be short, superficial, shallow, or selfish. Rather, God's Word will guide us into God's will, and this will become the delight of our hearts.

Join us now as we pray in one accord on Day 12 at www.acts413.net/21days or www.strategicrenewal.com/21days.

Day 13
Prayer Can Do Anything

Jim & Cathy Maxim

"Out of a very intimate acquaintance with [D. L. Moody] I wish to testify that he was a far greater pray-er than he was preacher. Time and time again, he was confronted by obstacles that seemed insurmountable, but he always knew the way to surmount and to overcome all difficulties. He knew the way to bring to pass anything that needed to be brought to pass. He knew and believed in the deepest depths of his soul that 'nothing was too hard for the Lord' and that **prayer could do anything that God could do**."[16]
—*R. A. Torrey*

"Now to Him who is able to do exceedingly abundantly above all that we ask or think, according to the power that works in us, to Him be glory in the church by Christ Jesus to all generations, forever and ever. Amen."
—Ephesians 3:20–21

---

16. R. A. Torrey, *D. L. Moody: Why God Used* (Editora Dracaena, 2015).

Anyone who has heard of D. L. Moody knows that he was a man with a ninth-grade education, a shoe salesman with no formal theological training of any kind. Yet God used him to shake the continents, found two Bible colleges, pastor a church with 8,000 members in Chicago, and write dozens of books. Most importantly, Moody was one of the greatest soul-winners of all time, and he knew that the obvious secret to his success was time in the secret place. He was well acquainted with the Almighty. "I'd rather be able to pray than to be a great preacher; Jesus Christ never taught his disciples how to preach but only how to pray," he once said.

There is a famous story about Moody told by Henry Varley, a British revivalist who had befriended Moody when he was in Dublin, Ireland, in 1873. A year after they met, Moody returned to Ireland for a Bible conference. He had become well known as an evangelist in America, and Varley recalled Moody's reason why God was blessing his ministry:

> During the afternoon of the day of conference Mr. Moody asked me to join him in the vestry of the Baptist Church. We were alone, and he recalled the night's meeting at Willow Park a year earlier and our converse the following morning.
>
> "Do you remember your words?" he said.
>
> I replied, "I well remember our interview, but I do not recall any special utterance."
>
> "Don't you remember saying, 'Moody, the world has yet to see what God will do with a man fully consecrated to him?'"

"Not the actual sentence," I replied.

"Ah," said Mr. Moody, "those were the words sent to my soul, through you, from the Living God. As I crossed the wide Atlantic, the boards of the deck of the vessel were engraved with them, and when I reached Chicago, the very paving stones seemed marked with 'Moody, the world has yet to see what God will do with a man fully consecrated to him.' Under the power of those words I have come back to England, and I felt that I must not let more time pass until I let you know how God has used your words to my inmost soul."[17]

Moody was a man consecrated to God who believed that prayer could do anything God could do. Paul, under the leading of the Holy Spirit, wrote it this way: "[God will do] *exceedingly abundantly above all that we can ask or think*" (Ephesians 3:20). He will do above all that we can ask or think. What is it that you are seeking from God? What's the true desire of your heart? Are you ready to ask God about it?

Notice when the exceedingly and abundantly comes—when we ask! When we talk with our Dad in heaven. Prayer can do anything God can do. Can you imagine what it would be like if we actually lived our lives this way? Would you like to know your heavenly Father more as your true best friend? D. L. Moody knew Him this way because he asked.

I will probably never be used in the powerful way D. L. Moody had been used. I will probably not start any colleges or be known around the world as a notable Christian leader. However,

---

17. Paul Gericke, *Crucial Experiences in the Life of D. L. Moody.*

I know that you and I have one thing in common with D. L. Moody: We have the same Father, and His promises to you and me are the same:

> *Ask, and it will be given to you; seek, and you will find; knock, and it will be opened to you. For everyone who **asks** receives, and he who **seeks** finds, and to him who **knocks** it will be opened. Or what man is there among you who, if his son asks for bread, will give him a stone? Or if he asks for a fish, will give him a serpent? If you then, being evil, know how to give good gifts to your children, how much more will your Father who is in heaven give good things to those who **ask Him!*** (Matthew 7:7–11)

This twenty-one days of fervent, intercessory prayer is all about learning to pray; learning to wait on God for the answer; learning that our part is to ask, seek, and knock; learning about how much our Dad in heaven wants to give us good things just as we want to give our kids good things. Most importantly, it's about learning how much spending time with our heavenly Father in the secret place changes us and changes our understanding of how He works for those who wait upon Him in prayer.

Join us in a prayer of agreement today. We will pray that our understanding will be opened, that we will know without a doubt that we can ask our heavenly Father to answer the desires of our hearts. We will also pray in earnest for our pastors, that they would be encouraged to believe that prayer can do anything that God can do in their churches and in their lives. Join us in prayer today on Day 13 at www.acts413.net/21days or www.strategicrenewal.com/21days.

Day 14
You Can Do Nothing

Jim Maxim

"Prayer is denouncing our own ability or natural capabilities
and engaging divine abilities that **know no limits**."
—*Jim Maxim*

*"I am the vine; you are the branches. Those who remain
[abide] in me, and I in them, will produce much fruit. For
apart from me **you can do nothing**."*
—John 15:5 (NLT)

Apart from me, Jesus said, *"you can do nothing."* No. Thing.

This is why we abide in Him, because God is the source of everything in our lives. In prayer, we willingly recognize Him as that source and transfer our concerns to His abilities. Now, I am not saying that we are supposed to sit back with our hands folded and let God do everything for us. As a Christian businessman who has been permitted to build an international company leading in its industry, I know for a fact that our God-given abilities are not supposed to just sit on the sidelines of life. We have been given a mind, body, and spirit to use to their maximum capabilities!

However, these abilities are a gift from God, and only He can usher us into their maximum force for His glory. Prayer and waiting on Him continue to keep us connected to Him and to His power source!

"Those who remain [abide] *in me, and I in them,* **will produce much fruit.** *For apart from me you can do nothing"* (John 15:5 NLT). Don't we want to bear much fruit for God's kingdom? That means leading others to Christ; praying for people who desperately need His hand; seeing your pastors encouraged and built up in their faith, your church growing spiritually and physically; and watching your loved ones come to Christ or perhaps be delivered from a bad situation or relationship. These twenty-one days of prayer show us exactly how to produce fruit in and around our lives—*we must abide in Jesus!*

Abiding in Jesus leads us to true intercession, the act of giving ourselves in prayer for the needs of others as well as ourselves. Intercession can set the captive free. Ephesians 6:18 encourages us to pray all the time, in all circumstances, for everyone we know who needs prayer! God wants us to pray that way because He understands that there is unlimited power in prayer.

R. A. Torrey wrote simply but profoundly, "Much prayer, much power. Little prayer, little power." The apostle Paul said the kingdom of God is not a matter of talk but of power! (See 1 Corinthians 4:20.)

This is the power that will change human lives eternally for the glory of almighty God when His Spirit is working through us. The Holy Spirit seeks God's children to empower them from on high, a power given to those who desire to glorify their Father in heaven. This power is available to all who ask in prayer, who are abiding and believing.

Praying, devoting ourselves to Him, fellowshipping with Him, honoring Him first every day, giving Him the first fruits of our time, becoming His friend, placing Him first in all we do, asking for His guidance first in everything, acknowledging that He alone is all powerful, agreeing with Him that apart from Him we can do nothing, asking Him to draw us closer daily, seeking a fresh touch from Him, acknowledging we love Him more than ourselves, acknowledging that He alone is holy and we are not, confessing our sins, asking for forgiveness, and being in right standing with Him—this is how we abide in Christ and how we bear the fruit we long to see growing in our lives and in the lives of those around us!

You can never have enough of God, and yet you can have as much of Him as you want! Let's seek the Lord together by praying in agreement to our faithful Father. Please visit www.acts413.net/21days or www.strategicrenewal.com/21days.

Day 15
Praying in Community

Daniel Henderson

"People ask, 'Which is more important—private prayer or corporate prayer?' The answer is yes. This is like asking, 'Which is more important for walking—your right leg or your left leg?'"
—*Daniel Henderson*

"*You also must help us by prayer, so that many will give thanks on our behalf for the blessing granted us through the prayers of many.*"
—2 Corinthians 1:11 (esv)

The early church understood the value of community, meeting together daily in prayer, and the other vital disciplines for spiritual growth. In Acts 2:42, we see the discipleship patterns that emerged in the Jerusalem church, comprised almost entirely of new believers. It says, *"And they continued steadfastly in the apostles' doctrine and fellowship, in the breaking of bread, and in the prayers."*

In the first century, you could not learn the apostle's doctrine by downloading a podcast. You had to be gathered in community. The same was true of fellowship and the breaking of bread. And how did they learn to pray? Together.

These prayers were not just a blessing tacked on to the beginning and end of Bible study. The early Christians gathered exclusively for prayer. In all likelihood, they followed the pattern Jesus set forth in the model prayer that led them through themes of worship, submission, intercession, supplication, warfare, and praise. In extended seasons of corporate prayer, they learned to pray effectively.

The church was birthed in a ten-day prayer meeting. (See Acts 1:14; 2:1.) They coped with crisis and persecution together on their knees. (See Acts 4:24–31.) As the church grew, the apostles refused to become embroiled in administrative problems because of their resolute desire to model prayer in their leadership team. (See Acts 6:4.) Through united prayer, they trusted God for miraculous, divine interventions in times of extreme trouble. (See Acts 12:5–12.) They received ministry direction through intense seasons of worshipful prayer. (See Acts 13:1–2.) In reality, early Christians learned to pray primarily by praying together. What a contrast to our individualized culture.

"Why have we neglected the corporate emphasis on prayer found in…Acts and the epistles?" asked Gene A. Getz, noted professor at Dallas Seminary, in his book *Praying for One Another*. In it, he shared how we have biased views of biblical prayer rather than an understanding of the original intent and context of the Scriptures. He noted that Western culture is distinguished by rugged individualism, and shared this observation:

> We use the personal pronouns "I" and "my" and "me." We have not been taught to think in terms of "we" and "our" and "us." Consequently, we individualize many references to corporate experience in the New Testament, thus often emphasizing personal prayer. More is said in Acts and the Epistles about corporate prayer, corporate learning of biblical truth, corporate evangelism, and corporate Christian maturity and growth than about the personal aspects of these Christian disciplines. Don't misunderstand. Both are intricately related. But the personal dimensions of Christianity are difficult to maintain and practice consistently unless they grow out of a proper corporate experience on a regular basis.[18]

Please don't misunderstand me—one-on-one time with the Lord in prayer is a precious gift that God has given to His children. Still, in Western culture, we have come to believe that it is enough to pray alone to the exclusion of others. This is a symptom of our basic view of society. In his book *The Connecting Church*, Randy Frazee described our culture of individualism. He noted that we are no longer born into a culture of community but a

18. Gene Getz, *Praying for One Another* (Wheaton, IL: Victor Books, 1983), 11.

"way of life that makes the individual supreme or sovereign over everything."[19] Frazee documented this as a problem, especially for those born after World War II. He lamented the effect it has on the church by observing that we have "all too often mirrored the culture by making Christianity an individual sport."[20]

Today, we read the commands about prayer in the New Testament Epistles and assume they are primarily designed to motivate the individual believer in his or her private prayer time. We have come to believe that prayer is first and best experienced at the private level. But we must keep in mind that until the advent of the printing press, almost all learning occurred in community settings. This clearly affected the way believers received and applied the truth. Today, with individual copies of the Bible, we make applications first, privately—then corporately, if at all.

In New Testament times, when a letter arrived from Paul, believers had but one chance to receive this truth. They had to show up. Period. And when a command was read in the original language, the plural pronouns popped. The application to believers as a community was clear. As a result, they prayed together often, passionately and obediently in agreement.

Michael Griffiths reiterated this consideration when he wrote,

> In standard English, the second person singular "you" and the second person plural "you" are identical. Thus, New Testament letters addressed to congregations are read (by us) as though they were addressed to the individuals. It is good and right that we should apply the

19. Randy Frazee, *The Connecting Church* (Grand Rapids, MI: Zondervan, 2001), 43.
20. Ibid., 85.

Scriptures to ourselves personally, but it is unfortunate if we also apply the Scriptures individualistically and ignore the fact that the original intention was to instruct us not so much as individuals, but as whole communities of Christian people.[21]

Today, many believers struggle to learn how to pray. Hundreds of volumes have been written on the theology and practice of prayer over the centuries. However, the most fundamental principle has often been neglected. Young Christians must learn to pray in community with mature believers. Prayer is vital for transformation, and corporate prayer is indispensable as a part of the process.

There are many reasons to pray together with other believers. We have already made it clear that prayer of agreement among Christians brings the presence and power of God to bear in the situation.

One of my other favorite reasons to pray together is noted in 2 Corinthians 1:11. Paul had been facing serious, even life-threatening, trials. Through it all, the Lord was bringing Paul to a new level of trust, but he knew that he still needed the prayers of the assembled church in Corinth, so he wrote, *"You also must help us by prayer, so that many will give thanks on our behalf for the blessing granted us through the prayers of many"* (2 Corinthians 1:11 ESV).

One of the reasons we must pray together for one another and for our church leaders is that it multiplies a greater expression of thanksgiving to God as we all participate in the process

---

21. Michael Griffiths, *God's Forgetful Pilgrims* (London: InterVarsity Press, 1978), 24.

and the glorious outcome of prayer. More have prayed and, as a result, more have recognized God's work and His answers.

So today, let us resolve to pray together often. While we are at it, let us make certain that we pray for our leaders so that our Lord may receive great expressions of thanksgiving for His work in the lives of our leaders and our churches. Join us for prayer on Day 15 at www.acts413.net/21days or www.strategicrenewal.com/21days.

Day 16

Extraordinary Love Found Me

Cathy Maxim

"Though our feelings come and go,
God's love for us does not."[22]
—C. S. Lewis

"**See what kind of** love the Father has given to us, that we
should be called children of God; and so we are."
—1 John 3:1 (esv)

"God, being rich in mercy, **because of the great love
with which he loved us**, even when we were dead in our
trespasses, made us alive together with Christ—by grace
you have been saved."
—Ephesians 2:4–5 (esv)

I often think about what it will be like when I first get to heaven. How overwhelmed and thankful I'll be! Will I see Jesus

---

22. C. S. Lewis, *The Complete C. S. Lewis Signature Classics* (New York: HarperCollins Publishers, 2002), 111.

first? What will it be like to be in the presence of the Father? Will I be able to sit at the Father's feet and feel loved like a young child with her parent? Then I think about who will be there waiting for me—my dad; my mother-in-law, Isobel; my brother, Charles, who died of kidney disease before I was born; my two grandmothers; and my great-grandma, aunts, uncles, friends, and other family members. But when I think of this, there is always one special person I can't wait to meet.

I want to meet the person who prayed for me. I know there is someone who prayed for me when I was first born. Maybe it was a nurse. I don't know who it was, but I know someone prayed, because my life has been extraordinary! I say extraordinary because of how the Lord has watched over me and how He came to me and reached down from heaven and revealed Himself to me.

Yes, extraordinary love found me! "This is my story, this is my song / Praising my Savior all the day long."[23] "I once was lost, but now am found, / Was blind, but now I see."[24] And I wonder who it was, who was obedient to Christ—who was this person who prayed for me?

How rich a testimony if this was said of each of us. If we could each say when that time came, "It was me—I prayed for you!" The greatest work we will ever do is pray for a soul to receive Christ.

Second Samuel 14:14 (NLT) says, "*God does not just sweep life away; instead, he devises ways to bring us back when we have been separated from him.*" I know this remote Scripture is talking about an entirely different situation, but the truth in the statement

---

23. Fanny Jane Crosby, "Blessed Assurance," 1873.
24. John Newton, "Amazing Grace," 1779.

speaks of God's heart and power to intervene in our loved ones' lives.

I also pray John 3:27 (NLT): *"No one can receive anything unless God gives it from heaven."* This Scripture reminds me that it's not my job to work change in people's hearts; it is God's job. I'm just asking Him to do it. Our prayers cover them in the process.

I ask the Lord to lift the blinders of sin over others' lives, and so I pray Isaiah 1:18: *"'Come now, let us reason together,' says the LORD, 'though your sins are like scarlet, they shall be as white as snow.'"* Sin distorts our thinking, so how can a person reason when they are blinded by their desire for sin? They need God's mighty intervention; we all need God's mighty intervention. They need their sins to be wiped clean, which happens miraculously because of the blood of Jesus Christ.

We need to believe that the Lord will do all that Ezekiel saw, so I pray Ezekiel 36:25–27 (NLT):

> *I will sprinkle clean water on you, and you will be clean. Your filth will be washed away…. And I will give you a new heart, and I will put a new spirit in you. I will take out you stony, stubborn heart and give you a tender, responsive heart. And I will put my Spirit in you so that you will follow my decrees and be careful to obey my regulations.*

Ask the Lord to give them the desire and understanding to pray, to confess that Jesus is their Lord and Savior, *"for all have sinned and fall short of the glory of God"* (Romans 3:23). *"For God so loved the world that He gave His only begotten Son, that whoever believes in Him should not perish but have eternal life"* (John 3:16).

Ask the Lord to give you fresh faith no matter the circumstances surrounding your loved ones. I know that praying God's

Word into the lives of those we love makes a difference because extraordinary love found me!

Join us now as we pray in faith agreeing for our loved ones— those in our families and in the family of God—that the Lord would release them from the blinders of sin, wash them white as snow, and set them free from all that is hindering their love for God.

Join us for prayer on Day 16 at www.acts413.net/21days or www.strategicrenewal.com/21days.

Day 17
Prayers of the Heart

Jim & Cathy Maxim

"Four things let us ever keep in mind: God hears
prayer, God heeds prayer, God answers prayer,
and God delivers by prayer."[25]
—E. M. Bounds

*"This is the confidence that we have in Him, that if we ask
anything according to His will, He hears us. And if we*
know *that He hears us, whatever we ask, we* ***know*** *that we
have the petitions that we have asked of Him.*
—1 John 5:14

Have you ever prayed a God-sized prayer? Can you remember a time when the intercession you made was so intense and so full of God's power that you knew for sure that God would

---

25. Edward McKendree Bounds, *Prayer and Praying Men* (London: Hodder & Stoughton, 1921), 63.

move the mountain? On a scale of one to ten, with ten being the highest, what number would you give your level of expectation? Be honest.

What would it look like to pretend that God would answer *all* your prayers and give you *the desires of your heart*? Take a moment right now and grab a clean sheet of paper. While no one else is looking, write down what you would ask God for if you knew without a doubt that He would answer that prayer. Remember, nobody is going to see it! You can shred it as soon as you are done with it.

Now, read it aloud to yourself. Does that list scare you or get you excited? Provided that the dream in your heart will glorify God, build up your faith, or bless other people, can the almighty God of the universe make that dream of yours come to pass? I'm sure He can.

Do you know that this is really hard for most people to do? It may be that they don't want to be disappointed with another failed dream. It may be that they are embarrassed by their prayers. Perhaps it seems as if nothing they ask for ever seems to happen, so they believe it is just a waste of time. They may believe that God doesn't really answer prayers that have to do with Him blessing us and using us for His glory. They believe that only special people get their prayers answered.

How do *you* feel about it? Let's consider the desires you wrote down, because I want to discuss them with you. I have walked with God for more than forty years. I have counseled hundreds of people and listened to thousands of people pray. During that time, I have discovered that most people do not believe that God is personally interested in them the way the Bible promises. They do not believe that God truly wants to listen to them or answer them as a loving Father would.

> *Blessed be the God and Father of our Lord Jesus Christ, who has blessed us with every spiritual blessing in the heavenly places in Christ, just as He chose us in Him...in love, having predestined us to adoption as sons by Jesus Christ to Himself, according to the good pleasure of His will.*
>
> (Ephesians 1:3–5)

Not believing this simple truth—that we are His children—is holding many back from entering into a deep relationship with God our Father and from getting answers to the prayers of their hearts.

How can we do greater works than Jesus (see John 14:12) if we don't believe God will meet us in our prayer closet? How can we be like the early disciples who *"turned the world upside down"* (Acts 17:6) if we don't trust Him to answer our prayers? How can He lead us to the perfect job or help us start our dream business or bless our ministry if we don't believe the promises in the Bible?

God is waiting for you to take Him at His Word. After all, the desires of your heart are His seeds planted there for your life, and you need to trust Him. Believe in the power He has placed in you—not in your own ability, but in His power—and take that step of faith. Remember, if we are not careful, we will pray only prayers that we can almost answer ourselves!

> Do not strive in your own strength; cast yourself at the feet of the Lord Jesus, and wait upon Him in the sure confidence that He is with you and works in you...strive

in prayer; let faith fill your heart; so will you be strong in the Lord and in the power of His might.[26]

Because you have dedicated yourself to these twenty-one days of fervent, agreeing prayer, I believe that your heart, your inner person, truly longs to connect more intimately with God the Father, Jesus His Son, and the Holy Spirit. I believe this journey we are walking together in prayer is God's gift to you. I know it has been for me.

Let us go to the Lord together in prayer on Day 17. We will pray fervently for the secret prayers of our hearts to be answered by the God who loves us and wants the best for our lives. We will also pray for our pastors and their families, that they would lift their hearts' desires in prayer to the Lord and trust Him to hear and answer them. Join us at www.acts423.net/21days or www.strategicrenewal.com/21days.

Day 18
Pray Without Ceasing

Jim & Cathy Maxim
"Prayer is not an exercise, it is the life."[27]
—*Oswald Chambers*

"Rejoice always, pray without ceasing, in everything give thanks; for this is the will of God in Christ Jesus for you."
—1 Thessalonians 5:16–18

---

26. Andrew Murray, *Andrew Murray on Prayer* (New Kensington, PA: Whitaker House, 1998).
27. Oswald Chambers, *My Utmost for His Highest*, classic ed. (Grand Rapids, MI: Discovery House, 2011).

"[Pray] at all times in the Spirit, with all prayer and
supplication. To that end, keep alert with all perseverance,
making supplication for all the saints."
—Ephesians 6:18 (esv)

Not many Christians remain all day, every day, in prayer on their faces, walking around with their heads down and hands clasped, or praying without interruption as they work, shop, or drive around town.

The concept of praying without ceasing is more closely related to an attitude or action of first response to everything in our lives. The Greek word for *"ceasing"* is *adialeiptos*, which translates "without omission." We should not be omitting prayer from any of life's situations, whether it's something simple or disastrous. As Paul said in Ephesians 6, we must stay alert, conditioning ourselves to pray first when life jumps out and interferes with our life plan. We should pray throughout the day as thoughts or needs arise, not limiting ourselves to a Wednesday night prayer group or a few quick minutes at the end of the day.

Our bodies do some things automatically, like emergency responses to sudden actions or noises. Why not condition our hearts to immediately respond in prayer in the same way? We should always be sensitive to the needs around us, never becoming too accustomed to the things that cry out for our intercession, like someone who lives in a big city and no longer hears the noises around him. We don't want to go through life observing people and events—obvious prayer needs—with no reaction on our part or with only a mental note to remember to pray for them at the next prayer meeting.

Pray without ceasing. What is our first reaction to a disappointment, crisis, tragedy, or success? Are we trusting in God all day, every day, or only when there is a disappointment, crisis, tragedy, or success? Do we pick up God in the morning and remember Him at night before bed?

Do we really believe that prayer changes things? Do we really believe that God intervenes in the affairs of men? If so, then why not pray without ceasing? If prayer is so important to us and to the rest of the world, then why don't we take every opportunity to pray, to pray empowered by the Holy Spirit at all times? If you are like me, you are saying yes to all these questions. If you are wondering how this can be done, we will look at it one step at a time.

Progress, not perfection, is what we are looking for. Let's start by looking at normal, everyday opportunities to pray and then how to build a life of continual prayer from there.

+ In the morning: Do you say, "It's morning, good god" or "Good God, it's morning"? Prayer as easy communication, or conversation, is directed, faith-building prayer!

+ Driving/commuting time: You can reclaim the time and get ready for the day in God's strength. You can pray for others who need God's grace and direction for their day as well. As I mentioned earlier, for years my prayer each morning has been, "Father God, in the name of Jesus, please use me today to make faith come alive in someone's heart, somewhere. Lord, please help me share Your love with somebody today."

+ Before any meal: Praying for food might seem like a ritual to some people. Why not just bless the food quickly and then get out your prayer list? There are note-taking applications for any cell phone! You don't need to pray for them all, just the top two, or the next two, as you bring prayer needs before the

Lord. Bless the president and our government leaders, bless your pastor and his family, three times a day, then watch out!

+ Every time you think of or hug your spouse, children or grandchildren: Pray a blessing upon their lives in the name of Jesus.

+ During any crisis: Retrain your senses to react in prayer first. I cannot recall when this first happened, but anytime I see an ambulance with lights on and sirens blaring, I pray that God will be glorified in the situation.

+ At night: Prayer can be more planned and quieter, more comprehensive and calming, and more unifying for married couples if they pray with their spouses.

Join us on Day 18 as we pray together for the Spirit to lead us in a continual life of prayer. Let's bring the needs of our leaders and those around us to the Lord as an integral part of our daily lives in the Spirit. Go to www.acts413.net/21days or www.strategic renewal.com/21days.

Day 19
A Praying Life

Daniel Henderson

"Prayer is not the only thing we do, just the first thing we do. It is not our last resort but our first response and our enduring resolve."
—Daniel Henderson

"So, from the day we heard, we have not ceased to pray for you, asking that you may be filled with the knowledge of his

> *will in all spiritual wisdom and understanding."*
> —Colossians 1:9 (ESV)

> *"Continue steadfastly in prayer, being watchful in it with*
> *thanksgiving."*
> —Colossians 4:2 (ESV)

Recently, while reading Paul's letter to the believers in Colossae, I was struck by a new thought. Over the years, I have always assumed that Paul simply prayed while he wrote the letter to the Colossians—which he obviously did as he was inspired by the Holy Spirit. But I could not help but wonder if, in fact, Paul wrote the letter out of the context of a prayer.

In a style fairly typical of Paul, he opens his letter to the Colossians with a reference to his prayers of thanks for these believers, which then leads him to actually write an extended prayer for them as the Spirit inspires him. (See Colossians 1:9–14.) This spiritual prayer sets the tone for the rest of the letter. Prayer framed the deep struggle he felt for them in his soul (see Colossians 2:1), which some commentators believe was primarily a struggle in his prayers on their behalf.

As Paul concluded the letter, he returned to the reality of prayer. You could say that he urged them to join him in prayer and hoped they will follow his example. He wanted them to do as he had done by praying for them as he had entreated the Lord for their spiritual blessings in an attitude of gratitude. As he concluded, he gave this challenge, *"Continue steadfastly in prayer, being watchful in it with thanksgiving"* (Colossians 4:2 ESV).

So we discover that prayer was interlaced throughout the letter to the Colossians because it was woven so deeply in Paul's heart as he wrote. His writing and his leading were evidences of his pursuit of Christ and lifestyle of prayer.

Too often, we arrange our praying around our regular activities rather than arranging our other activities around our praying. Perhaps we view prayer as a separate "compartment" in our routine rather than the moment-by-moment compulsion of our daily life. Paul's model reminds us that prayer shapes the very environment and content of all we do and is the fuel for our daily spiritual passion.

My friend Pastor Keeney Dickenson once noted, "We tend to pray in the context of ministry. Jesus ministered in the context of prayer." In today's lifestyle, we can easily draw a firm line between prayer and Bible study. We see a clear distinction between prayer and ministry activity. This is often seen in our tradition of opening and closing our gatherings in prayer. Perhaps for Jesus and Paul, that line was virtually indiscernible. Prayer was not about some obligatory duty attached to specific responsibilities but rather a pulsating spiritual desire that permeated all things in life.

So what might happen if we lived, related, worked, and served in the context of a praying life? No doubt we would be much more aware of the presence, power, and promises of the Holy Spirit. Our orientation in daily life would be eternal, not temporal. If we lived a praying life, the loudest voice of the day would not be our own emotions or the opinions of men but rather the will of the Holy Spirit. We would be able to better obey His promptings, speak His truth, and boldly witness to others of His gospel. We would live a life of sufficiency rather than focusing on our own scarcity. Abiding prayer would change every reasoning of the mind, every relationship in the home, and every reaction to life's challenges.

So today, ask the Holy Spirit to give you a deepening conviction, a fresh consciousness, and a renewed commitment to abide in Christ through a praying life.

Let's pray for our church leaders in the same way. Let's ask the Lord to give them a greater sense of the role of prayer in daily life, relationships, decisions, and service of the flock. Join us as we pray together on Day 19 at www.acts413.net/21days or www.strategicrenewal.com/21days.

Day 20
Prayer Is the Right Thing

Daniel Henderson

"Talking to men for God is a great thing, but talking to
God for men is greater still."[28]
—E. M. Bounds

*"I appeal to you, brothers, by our Lord Jesus Christ and
by the love of the Spirit, to strive together with me in your
prayers to God on my behalf, that I may be delivered from
the unbelievers in Judea, and that my service for Jerusalem
may be acceptable to the saints, so that by God's will I may
come to you with joy and be refreshed in your company.
May the God of peace be with you all. Amen."*
—Romans 15:30–33 (esv)

The apostle Paul relied heavily on the prayers of the churches for his ministry. (See 2 Corinthians 1:8–11; Ephesians 6:18–19;

---

28. E. M. Bounds, *E. M. Bounds on Prayer* (Peabody, MA: Hendrickson Publishers, 2006), 115.

Colossians 4:2–4; 1 Thessalonians 5:25; 2 Thessalonians 3:1.) In Romans 15, he described his plans to deliver a love offering to the beleaguered Jewish believers in Jerusalem as he completed his collections among the Gentile churches. After his visit to Jerusalem, he hoped to visit the believers in Rome, then travel to Spain to preach the gospel. Knowing the spiritual battle that surrounded him in all those ministry endeavors, Paul urged the believers in Rome to pray for him, with specific instruction on how and what to pray as they engaged in their most strategic investment of focused intercession.

We can do the right things for the wrong reasons. Prayer is the right thing to do. Paul gave us solid reasons for our obedient intercession. Paul began this appeal by saying, *"I appeal to you, brothers…"* (Romans 15:30 ESV). He used the Greek term *parakaleo*, which means "to call to one's side."[29] As he did in 1 Timothy 2:1–3, Paul urged Christians to intercede for leaders. Knowing it is our duty to do so, we should pray for the leaders of the church.

Beyond mere duty, we must have overarching desire. This desire is rooted in our esteem and worship of Christ. Paul compelled believers to pray *"by our Lord Jesus Christ"* (Romans 15:30 ESV). Not only are we able to pray by Christ's provision (see Hebrews 7:25; 10:20–22), but we are also motivated to pray because of Christ's person—His glory, His name, and His renown.

Paul also called us to pray *"by the love of the Spirit"* (Romans 15:30 ESV). The most literal rendering of this is "by your love for the Holy Spirit."[30] Our love for the person and power of the Holy

---

29. W. E. Vine, *Vine's Expository Dictionary of Biblical Words* (Nashville: Thomas Nelson, 1988)

30. John MacArthur, *The MacArthur Study Bible* (Nashville, TN: Nelson Bibles, 2006), 1691.

Spirit motivates us to pray for the demonstration of the Spirit in the lives and ministries of our spiritual leaders.

Paul continued urging believers to *"strive together with* [him] *in* [their] *prayers to God on* [his] *behalf."* This reflects the intense nature of prayer due to the seriousness of the spiritual battle we face. He calls on his friends in Rome and on us to contend with spiritual adversaries as we fight on our knees. (See 1 Corinthians 9:25; 1 Timothy 4:10; 6:12; 2 Timothy 4:7; Colossians 4:12.)

Paul then specified three key prayer requests. First, he requested *"that* [he] *may be delivered from the unbelievers in Judea"* (Romans 15:31 ESV). He is referring to hostile Jews who hated Paul and wanted to murder him. His journey back to Jerusalem was risky because he would face chains and tribulations. (See Acts 20:22–24.) Our spiritual leaders today may not face human persecution as Paul did, but the devil constantly bombards them with dangers, toils, and snares. We must pray for their protection.

In his second request, Paul asked the believers to pray *"that my service for Jerusalem may be acceptable to the saints"* (Romans 15:31 ESV). As we noted, he was bringing a love gift from Gentile believers to Jewish Christians in Jerusalem. Knowing the division, distrust, and prejudice that existed in that day, he was taking a risk—his gift might be rejected, or his motives questioned. He needed prayer for the Lord to make hearts receptive and bless this ministry effort. We must pray for the prosperity of the ministry efforts of our leaders.

Third, Paul requested prayer so *"that by God's will* [he] *may come to* [them] *with joy and may be refreshed in* [their] *company"* (Romans 15:32 ESV). Knowing the trials and strain of his leadership assignment, Paul asked them to pray for his joy and refreshment in their midst when he arrived. We, too, must pray for the Lord's provision in the hearts and souls of our church leaders.

The results of these prayers on Paul's behalf are chronicled in Acts 21:15–28:31. The Jewish believers gladly received this gift of love. (See Acts 21:17.) Then God used the Roman government to protect Paul from the murderous plots of the Jewish opponents. (See Acts 21:30–23:24.) God also protected Paul from shipwreck and a snakebite when he eventually traveled to Rome. (See Acts 27:1–28:16.) While under house arrest in Rome, many believers came to Paul and likely refreshed him, as is specifically described in the faithful encouragement of a man named Onesiphorus. (See 2 Timothy 1:16.)

So what can we expect as we pray for our leaders in this way? Certainly, we should watch for God-ordained answers in the lives of our leaders, but we also can expect that *"the God of peace be with* [them] *all"* (Romans 15:33 ESV). As we earnestly pray for the needs and ministries of our spiritual leaders, we will come to know the God of peace and experience the peace of God in our hearts and in our midst.

> *Do not be anxious about anything, but in everything by prayer and supplication with thanksgiving let your requests be made known to God. And the peace of God, which surpasses all understanding, will guard your hearts and your minds in Christ Jesus.*   (Philippians 4:6–7 ESV)

What a blessing to learn to pray based on this passage and to join the Lord in His paramount work of spreading the gospel through His leaders and His church. Join us today as we pray together at www.acts413.net/21days or www.strategicrenewal.com/21days.

Day 21
God's Will Is to Answer

Jim & Cathy Maxim

"Prayer delights God's ear; it melts his heart; and opens
his hand. God cannot deny a praying soul."[31]
—Thomas Watson

"I tell you, ask, and it will be given to you; seek, and you
will find; knock, and it will be opened to you. For everyone
who asks receives, and the one who seeks finds, and to the
one who knocks it will be opened."
—Luke 11:9–10 (ESV)

When we are praying, we should never feel as if we are twisting God's arm or overcoming God's reluctance to help us. It is God's will to answer our prayers. Remember that the Word of God tells us, *"This is the confidence that we have in Him, that if we ask anything according to His will, He hears us. And if we know that He hears us, whatever we ask, we know that we have the petitions that we have asked of Him"* (1 John 5:14–15). Your Father God longs to give you the desires of your heart. God longs to bless you. He longs to walk closely with you.

Remember that God is a Father who wants to listen to and answer His children. Jesus assured us, *"If you then, being evil, know how to give good gifts to your children, how much more will your Father who is in heaven give good things to those who ask Him!"*

---

31. Thomas Watson, *The Godly Man's Picture* (Zeeland, MI: Reformed Church Publications, 2009), 98.

(Matthew 7:11). Of course, we know this doesn't mean that everything we ever want is God's will for our lives, but it does mean that as our prayers line up with His Word and His will, He will answer them in His power and strength.

Jesus encouraged His disciples to pray in every possible way. *"Until now you have asked nothing in My name. Ask, and you will receive, that your joy may be full"* (John 16:24). *"Whatever you ask in My name, that I will do, that the Father may be glorified in the Son. If you ask anything in My name, I will do it"* (John 14:13–14).

In the Old Testament, God told us over and over again that His desire was to listen and answer our prayers: *"Then you will call upon Me and go and pray to Me, and I will listen to you"* (Jeremiah 29:12). *"I call upon you, for you will answer me, O God; incline your ear to me; hear my words [prayer]"* (Psalm 17:6 esv).

R. A. Torrey wrote, "God has not changed; and His ear is just as quick to hear the voice of real prayer, and His hand is just as long and strong to save, as it ever was."[32]

The Bible also says, *"Without faith it is impossible to please Him, for he who comes to God must believe that He is, and that He is a rewarder of those who diligently seek Him"* (Hebrews 11:6). Why would the writer of Hebrews say that? Because it is God's very nature to answer the cries of our souls. God knows how weak we are. He knows how much we need Him. He longs for you to have the kind of faith that cries out to Him daily and believes with all your heart that the things you ask Him will be done.

Prayer is simple. It is supernatural, a mysterious moral working of the Holy Spirit, but it is not logical. To anyone not related to our Lord Jesus Christ, prayer looks foolish, seeking someone

---

32. R. A. Torrey, *The Power of Prayer and the Prayer of Power* (New York: Cosimo Publications, 2009), 17.

who is unseen. However, we know that He hears us. It definitely requires faith to pray.

It has been said that no man, no matter how great his intellect, is greater than his prayer life. God longs to revive our prayer life. God longs to pour out the Holy Spirit inside of us in such a supernatural way that we want to run to Him every day and be with Him in prayer, to praise Him and to worship Him. God longs to have that intimate fellowship with us. God is so good!

As we have prayed together in agreement during these twenty-one days, we have the assurance that God has heard our prayers. It has been an honor and a pleasure to join together with you in your prayers.

If situations that seem overwhelming or impossible to you remain in your life, or if you don't have someone who will pray with you regularly, we encourage you to reach out to a local pastor. Reach out to a local church, especially one that believes in the power of prayer to change lives. The church of Jesus Christ is there to love you, encourage you, and bless you.

Join us on Day 21, our final day together, as we praise God for His faithfulness in that He hears us and answers our prayers! Let's go to Him in thankfulness because He has built up our faith! Let's also pray the prayer of agreement for one another and for our pastors and leaders, and that our faith in God's answer to prayer would grow continually. To God be the glory! Great things He has done! Join us at www.acts413.net/21days or www.strategicrenewal.com/21days.

About the Authors

Nearly forty years ago, Jim Maxim was at the lowest point of his life. As he lay at death's door, Jim's mother prayed for his soul. God answered her prayer and Jim's life was claimed, redeemed, and transformed for Jesus Christ. The dramatic story of Jim's conversion is found in his book, "Face-to-Face with God."

Jim served in the US Marine Corps and created multiple successful companies within the automotive industry. While working as an entrepreneur, he served God in prison ministries, as a speaker, and as a board member of ministries like Hope Pregnancy Center, the Valley Forge Leadership Prayer Breakfast, and others.

In 2011, Jim and his wife, Cathy, founded Acts413 Ministries, where they evangelize, counsel, and minister in the name of Jesus all over the world. In particular, Jim has been burdened to pray and lead others in intercessory prayer for pastors, their families, and churches.

The highlight of Acts413 Ministries is city-wide prayer gatherings held throughout the United States. They serve as a catalyst to mobilize the body of Christ to intercede for our pastors and their families. Christians from every denomination, socioeconomic background, culture, and color worship and pray through scripture in the name of Jesus Christ. While the prayers may cover many topics, there is always a special focus on interceding for pastors, their families, and churches. Jim firmly believes that the church is the primary plan for ministering to God's people on earth.

The Maxims have three sons, three daughters-in-law, and three grandchildren.

~

As a senior pastor for over two decades, Daniel Henderson brought prayer-based revitalization to numerous churches. Now, as the President of Strategic Renewal, he is dedicating his full-time efforts to help congregations across the country and world experience renewal.

Daniel is sought after for his expertise in leading corporate prayer. He has authored numerous books on biblical leadership and prayer including, Old Paths, New Power and Transforming Prayer: How Everything Changes When You Seek God's Face.